CONTENT

CHAPTER 1

Easdale

G lasgow in the 1950s was one of Britain's main industrial cities. It was full of hardworking people that made huge ships on the River Clyde. Train engines all over the world were also made in the city. It was full of beautiful buildings, with shop owners selling just about everything. Various transport workers, woodworkers making furniture, miners working deep underground, and steel workers combined to make a huge workforce that sustained industry in the United Kingdom and afar.

Queen Victoria visited Glasgow in 1849. She arrived by steam yacht at the Broomielaw and left the same day by train to Perth. She never thought much of the place and missed a great opportunity to really get to know the city and its wonderful people (the majority who had contributed to the wealth of her country).

In this wee book I write about a city I love, and the people who are full of humour (like Billy Connolly). It is a place of sadness and happiness, trauma, and interest like no other city in the world. Some of the names in the book have been altered to give them privacy. Here is my story.

Life's beginnings

They say we plan our destiny in heaven as spiritual beings, and everything on earth is a theatre, where the people we meet are from previous lives, all this to advance our souls, teaching us to love and forgive. This may well be true or not. I must have chosen Glasgow as my base camp, and it looked like my soul had a lot to learn.

I first made my entrance in the Glasgow Southern General Hospital, situated in the south side of the city not far from a major sewage works. My mother described my entrance as, "Like a good dose of Castor Oil". This was her view of labour pains. Due to ill health, she was unable to care for me post-natal, so I was whisked away to my lovely gran and Aunt Eileen in Easdale where both looked after me for which I am most grateful. I was told I was there for only 8 Months, but there are photos of me aged 2 on Easdale. Anyway, it was a long time ago. Easdale is 16 miles south of Oban on the west coast of Scotland. It's a charming, picturesque place, where a lot of tourists come to visit it and turn it into a busy spot in summer.

There was a story my dad told me about a tourist who arrived there before the war and asked a local where the toilets were. The answer shocked the poor woman, he said, "Och, just go down the shore behind a rock and put a stone on it". Toilets didn't appear until years later on the island.

My grandfather who owned fishing rights then as a salmon fisher-man, would go out to take in his nets in early morning. He would sail past a row of bare bottoms. These were locals with their own loo spot on the shore doing their business. If it was nowadays, they would all be arrested. They thought it hygienic as the tide cleaned it away every day.

My grandparents met while my grandmother came arrived on holiday to Easdale. She fell in love with the local fisherman and married him against her family's wishes. She was from upper class Glasgow, Edminston Drive. Maids, electric lights, and more. In those days you married for money and security, this was real love at its best. Grandad, whom I never met, was a hard worker, fishing in all weather, he had a shed which is still on the island, his name was above it, "Donald MacQueen". He did joiner work, made the coffins for the departed, made rowing boats for the gentry in their large estates. He got £500 for a boat sale, that was a fortune then.

My grandmother, Agnes Sutherland, had eight babies all born in a small cottage with no running water or electricity, an outside toilet was a bucket in a shed, with a paraffin heater only in it. They brought their family up as church going every Sunday, that meant dressing all the children smart, taking the boat to the mainland, and then a walk of a mile to get to the small church on Ellenabeich.

Grandad was a church elder and a great singer. He would be the introducer of the hymns.

Word went around the district that a film crew were going to look for extras. Each would be paid £5 (that was a lot then). Then the locals discovered it was to happen on the Sabbath, well, that was shocking they all agreed as they would be in church. Come the Sunday filming day only two families were present--my grandparents and another couple.

To know where your family came from is such a wonderful thing. It gives you roots and foundation for your life journey. Today we have ancestry web sites and more to discover our family history, but when it is told by the elderly in a family, it becomes part of who you are as a person. I watch these programs where siblings meet up with those they never knew existed and it is heartwarming. They are ecstatic to meet for the first time after years of nothing. It does make me grateful for all my aunts, cousins, uncles, and grandparents. To have known them and loved them, even though a lot of them have gone on ahead of me in the spiritual world.

After my short stay in Easdale and leaving my aunt and gran behind, my dad brought me back to live with him and my mum in a small flat in Paisley. We were there for only a couple of years until my wee sister was born, dear Anna three years younger than me, my very best friend.

The fact there was an age gap meant we didn't really connect until we were older.

The family moved to 45 Clifford Street, just across from the old Bellahouston School. The area at that time was called Ibrox, although my gran always called it Bellahouston, it sounded better she thought.

The Clifford Street house was at the bottom of a tenement. It contained a large kitchen with bed recess, a bedroom for my sister and I, a sitting room, bathroom with bath, toilet, and sink. I mention these plumbing items as a lot of flats in Glasgow at the time didn't have them. Some still had toilets outside, or in the close for sharing with 6 families. Our home was one of the lucky few. My dad got a mortgage for £1,200. This he paid monthly for years on his meagre wage of £15 a month. Electric and gas were cheaper than today. They paid rates to the council for bin collections, which were only our ashes from the one coal fire. Rubbish was burned there, clothes were handed to other children, and life was simple but happy.

My father, my hero, trained as a cabinet maker in Paisley at college. He got a job at William Morris in Milton Street, Glasgow making very upmarket furniture. He had been a prisoner of war in Germany who was taken at Dunkirk during the Second World War. He spent 5 long years in a German prison camp and didn't speak a lot about his experience. There was one story he told us about a fellow prisoner who would mock him for reading his bible, saying what rubbish was in it. A short time after they had marched 40 miles to the prison camp, and all lay down exhausted afterwards and had nothing to eat or drink for so long. The chap who mocked him sat next to him and said, "Give me a look at your bible."

My dad handed it to him, and after some time he turned to chat about how the read was. The man was stone dead. It was such a shock to everyone as he was a huge build, looked healthy and well fed, but God had another plan.

Another POW story was at Christmas in the camp, one of the guards got up in front of the prisoners and sang "Silent Night" in German. He did not speak any English, and he sang with tears in his eyes and great gusto. At the final clap from the audience a voice from

4

the back shouted, "Well done Hans, that was hellish". The hall erupted with huge laughter. Poor Hans thought it was a compliment.

After the war my dad returned to his highland home weighing only six and a half stone, looking so bad that not even his father and brother--who met him off the train at Oban-- knew who he was. His life would be plagued with ill health, and he was told he had a genetic heart condition and never should have been accepted as A1 for the army. His regiment, The Argyll and Southern Highlanders, owed him so much. He tried to get a pension from them when he became very unwell in later years, but sadly lost the tribunal in Edinburgh. Consequently, poverty plagued my childhood.

Food was always respected in our house, nothing wasted, and only tea biscuits as a treat. We did get a good meal after school and during secondary I got school dinners, a godsend to me. My mum's cooking was basic. I could tell you what I had to eat any day in my childhood. Mince Monday, fish Tuesday, sausages Wednesday, and so it went. Never an alteration of the menu from one week to the next.

One of the promises I made to my father to carry out his wishes, was to always shake hands with a German, to let them know that their people was forgiven by him and that the young generation were never responsible for the war in which many died.

My mother, born in Oban, went to Oban High School. Her mother was from Perth, her father's family were from Ardnamurchan on the West Coast. John Cameron owned The Mart in Oban, a shop at Connel, land at McCaigs tower for sheep, and the Isle of Shuna. He was a farmer and the boss of the home. They had five children. One died young, David. He was never well and died as a baby. The story was that my grandparents went on a visit to Perth to see relations. They got the train, then my grandad being thrifty hired a public carriage. They sat next to a dirty looking mother and child. The child had German Measles (Rubella). It causes health problems in babies. My gran was pregnant at the time, and she never forgave my grandad for putting her alongside these "Dirty People". Poor wee David didn't have a chance of life.

My mother was in the ATS (Auxiliary Territorial Army) during the war. She was put on the telephones due to her sweet-sounding highland accent. Everyone from all parts of the UK understood it. She guided the planes of the RAF over the channel. There was always sadness when one of the pilots did not return, but a joy when she heard those who survived return.

I was told when very young after coming home from school and singing "The Skye Boat Song". Mum told me not to be singing that song in this house. Seemingly my very great grandfather on my mother's side fought at Culloden as a Cameron Jacobite. He escaped butchering by running away for his life. My mum said he told all the family he was nearly killed with the fault of that clown Charlie.

It must have been very hard for young women being taken from a job that was pleasant and easy (mum worked in the Chinese Shop in Oban) to be flung in at the deep end doing such a responsible job with people's lives in your hands. I never found out about what she did during wartime until an aunt told me years later. Maybe her illness after my birth was depression brought on by her work in the army. She was plagued with depression most of her life, a lot of the times she ended up in Leverndale Hospital which made home life difficult for my dad. He would end up in the Southern General with his heart condition. Thankfully my sister and I were never taken into care as their hospital stays didn't overlap. Money was tight most of the time.

Mum worked in Gemmel's Shop on Gower Street. She loved her work there. One time the boss left her in charge of the shop and to lock up at night. That night she couldn't manage to turn the lock so ran across the road to my dad for help. Anna and I were given strict instructions to stand at the window where they could watch us from the shop, we were about 10 and 7 years old. We stood and gazed at both our parents being put into a police car. A neighbour thought they were burglars and phoned the police. I was puzzled but we still stood at the window. It must have been an hour later when they came home by the police car outside our close. I'm sure it gave them a shock.

I never got free sweets from that shop. We were not allowed sweets during weekdays just to protect our teeth was the excuse. It was more like they couldn't afford it. I didn't get pocket money until I was 12. I got a penny for every year of my life amounting to one shilling. That was magic. I could buy Parma Violets, Lucky Potatoes, Lovehearts, Toffee Caramels, McGowans Toffee, Sherbet Fountain the whole lot of goodies. I was in heaven.

Saturday night was bath night. The fire was built up with huge amount of coal. Bags of Coal were 10/6p a bag then. It was our only heat in the kitchen and the centre of the house. Dross, which was the dregs of coal that had crumbled at the bottom, was piled on top of the huge flame. It all heated the boiler at the back giving plenty hot water for the bath to be filled. My sister and I were first in to get scrubbed down and hair washed.

Dad carried out the washing of us when very young, and we did the washing and he supervised in case we drowned, "Don't forget your neck and between your toes", he would say. Pears soap was the only thing for a lather, then we would run to the kitchen to dry ourselves in front of the fire. Mum would go in next, lastly dad all in the same water. We were clean compared to other kids. Most children then didn't have baths and certainly never showers.

We were checked for nits and lice in our hair with a wee fine comb. I once caught them from a school friend, my parents went nuts about it, calling names of disgust about the great unwashed in my class, which was true. The poor wee souls, some of them stank to high heaven. Some of them never had their hair combed from day to day. One wee girl was sent home she was so mucky and smelling of urine. Our family were clean compared to others. I felt different to my classmates with my soap scented hair and powdered body, clean underwear and ironed blouse. I was aware that a lot of the kids were badly treated at home with bruises to show for it.

Then came the haircut night. Once a month dad would sharpen the one pair of household scissors. We would be sat down at his feet, and he would proceed to chop at our hair. One night, poor Anna got her ear clipped by mistake and there was a great stramash of yelling and blood over her shoulder. Dad apologized but blamed her for wriggling around. The horrendous fringe was then cut (always squint), then for the final flourish a razor was taken to the nape of the neck as a tidy up.

The end look was like Friar Tuck on a bad day. I had been given at birth a huge mop of wild curly hair, looking like a wee African baby. It grew wilder as I grew, so in his wisdom dad took me to a posh shop (Pettigrew's I think) where it was straightened and cut to a bob style costing the whole of five pounds (a fortune then). All so dad could cut it himself and save money on future hairdressers. When I turned 15 years old, I announced to dad that I was growing my hair long. I could

7

see the horror in his face, saying, "But you look so smart with it short." I could sit on my hair a year later.

Our house was in a close, the walking area for all to gain access to their homes, three stories high, six houses in all. I had only seen the basement area once in my life. It was huge wooden supports holding up the giant stones above. I had gone to show an apprentice plumber where the water pipes were, we had a leak, the guy came to the door when my dad had left for a few minutes to get cigarettes. He asked me for a "Connel". This left me confused. I was about 10 at the time, Dad came home and heard the request. Connel is Glaswegian for candle.

The close was always a happening place. The Manson family stayed next door. They had three girls. Mrs. Manson was lovely and good looking. A super baker, she worked as a cook in a local children's home. She was from Barra and spoke with a beautiful highland voice. Her husband John was disabled after a back injury. He managed the family chores while she worked. They were good neighbours, and often Mrs. Manson would bake cakes and offer us one when out the back green.

Above them were the Tremels, an elderly couple with no family. Mr. Tremel was a very strange wee man. He wore a jazzy looking waistcoat of many bright colours, horned rimmed glasses and baldy head. He always looked flustered and stressed darting his head in all directions as though a bee was chasing him. Mrs. Tremel was the local nosy parker. She would peek out from behind her curtains every time a door was shut in the close. The original CT camera and neighbourhood watch, we used to look up for her. Sure enough, there she was hiding behind the green curtain, taking everything in and listening for gossip. She used to invite the local police up for tea and scones, no doubt gathering all the local information. The FBI would have been proud of her.

At Halloween we would be invited in as children dressed up for the occasion, she would ask what mum and dad were up to. I was naughty and cottoned on to her nosy ways. I was about 10 and could make up great stories of rubbish about my parents, one being, "Oh, mum and dad were sunbathing in front the fire last night", or "Dad won the football pools and got a lot of money". The delight in her face at this information made me have a laugh to myself. They had no family. She told my mum the reason was that her "Hole was too wee", hence poor Mr. Tremels frustrated look. I think he was what they now call a pedophile. He got himself a new green car, the only one in the street, and they drove a hundred yards to the local church, "Just to show off" my dad said.

One day he asked if Anna and I would like a run to the park, and there was about six of us kids crammed into the car. We loved it and waved to all the passersby. At the park he asked me if I would come to look at the bushes with him. It was Maxwell Park and there were beautiful rhododendron bushes there. I sniffed a rat and said, "No way, I'll stay here with my pals". I ran down to the rest of the kids and quietly told them what he said. We all stuck together; he sat on a bench glowering at all of us. Thankfully we all got home safe, never again.

They had a nephew, Cuddles, Mrs. T called him. He was about 14. When I was 8 years old, he was worldly wise about all things I had never heard of. Sex was something I never knew about, even at nursing college. I could name all the anatomical parts of the human body, I had watched the birth of a baby on TV, "Your life in their hands", but as an innocent child I never knew the bits fitted into each other to make a little human. This came as a complete shock to me, especially when Judy, one my college friends, showed me my first Durex. I didn't know what the heck it was. She explained in graphic detail where it went, what its purpose was, how to put it on, and its disposal.

After that I looked at my parents with great suspicion and horror, thinking that's how I came into this world. I was 16 years old and had a lot to learn I thought, but no boy is doing THAT to me. She never explained it was great fun, a feeling of wonder and such a natural thing to happen. It was not for me, animal-like, dirty, and not correct way to behave. These things went through my innocent empty head. I fell out with Judy after that. I thought what a way to lead your life.

Anyway, getting back to Cuddles, he told us that all the girls where he stayed stripped naked and walked up and down to show their bodies to the boys in the area. I thought what a bunch of nutcases. Us Scottish girls refused his request to strip off for him, thank goodness. His next request was to me, before my appendix was removed, I had a mole on my right side. This detail I stupidly mentioned to Cuddles as we all discussed birth marks one day.

For weeks after he ask to see my mole. It went on and on day after day. I refused point blank, then one day to shut him up, I said, "Ok, close your eyes". Cuddles stood with eye lids tight shut. At that I began

9

to arrange my clothing so that only the mole would be viewed. Just at that, a loud voice came through the close, "Iona MacQueen, you behave yourself". It was Mrs. Manson. She had heard the discussion and was protecting me from the mad Cuddles. I was so delighted to be saved from this awful boy, that's how it was then. Neighbours looked out for other kids as well as their own. We were like one big family. Mrs. Tremel had her faults like all of us, but she was a tremendous singer. She should have been on stage she was so good, and on summer days we could hear her singing her heart out with her window open, we all listened intently as children.

My mother never discussed anything about sex, but said, "Protect yourself from boys." Periods were skimmed over. A story was told about some poor female who menstruated at a dance, and all the women went around her to shelter her saying she sat on a strawberry.

Above the Tremel Couple were the Pardace family. He was from Italy, his wife a Scot. They had three girls with fabulous Italian names Sabrina, Armanda and Marcia. All of them had dark brown eyes, long hair with ribbons tied through it, not like my Friar Tuck job. Then later came a son named after the great artist of Italy Leonardo da Vinci. The boy was also very good looking with sallow skin colour, brown eyes and curly brown hair.

The father took them all to Italy on holiday most years, a huge undertaking with four children and his poor exhausted wife. They drove through the Alps on dangerous roads that were very narrow. One story he told was when he asked his wife to light a ciggy for him, she put it in his mouth the wrong way around, the car swerved and they nearly all went down the cliffs. Thankfully he managed to keep on the road a gulped some water to cool his mouth.

The other great excitement was when he took his daughter on a fishing boat from Ayr to the sea. It was just a rowing boat, no lifejackets, and off they sailed. He never checked the weather forecast for the day ahead. Things got wild and stormy as they got out into the Atlantic. It was getting dark. His daughter then took a hissy fit of fear and tried to jump overboard, he then tied her to the boat which made her worse, but he said he did it to save her life. Eventually they reached the shores of Arran when darkness fell. They both crawled out on to the shore and were rescued by some locals. They were very lucky indeed.

The newspaper people interviewed them next day, as did the police. The whole thing sounded to us children like something from an American film, and we were also horrified thinking of what they went through.

Mr. P said he worked in the Shieldhall Sewage Works. I said to him, "That's a dirty job is it not? "Oh no, not at all", was the answer. "We all wear white coats. It's very clean and there are beautiful flower beds." Some years later while I was at nursing college, I visited the very place he had worked at. It was minging (a Glasgow word for dirty), and the whole area stank to high heaven, and not one white coat in sight. No sign either of Mr. P. He was maybe in the flower beds.

Across from the Pardace family were the Ingles Family. The father worked for the Evening Times. One time when I was very young, I wrote my Santa letter. I requested to have twins, meaning dolls, my dad took the letter to Mr. Ingles and he had it printed in his newspaper. The piece said, "What will dad do, he has to move quick before Christmas." My dad thought this hilarious, and I hadn't a clue what he was on about.

I never saw Mr. Ingle's wife or can remember her, but there was a daughter. Her husband was at sea, and she had a baby I recall. She worked in a biscuit factory as a supervisor. If couples had no children, then not much was known about them, as all we kids played together out the back greens, and children have no secrets between each other. Every kid knew every parent in the block and every detail about them. Even bra sizes and knicker sizes were up for discussion and giggles, as washing was hung outside to dry near our play areas.

Above us were the two elderly ladies, Miss McInnes, and Miss Steven. They seemed very old to us. I didn't know much about them, and they kept to themselves. My dad would go upstairs often to check they were ok. He suggested that if either of them needed help they could just knock down to us. One night my family were all sitting by the fire discussing school or some other boring stuff, when dad shouted, "Quiet girls". We all heard a knock, faint but rat a tat-tat. Dad rushed upstairs, no answer from the door, so he called the police. When the police opened the door, they found poor Ms. Steven on the floor with a broken leg. She had fallen badly and had to be taken to the hospital. She recovered well and was most grateful to my dad for saving her.

It was the talk of the back green and such a heroic story. We knew nearly all the folk around us, maybe not by name, but to say "Hello" to or just a wee wave. We were taught at home that it was rude not to recognise people when we see them, but also never to go into their house unless mum said, never to speak to folk we didn't know, and that advice saved me from an awful situation when I was about 10 years old.

I was playing out the front on the pavement with my Hula Hoop, working furiously at it spinning around my skinny waist, when a car stopped beside me and a man reached over to offer me a sweet from a bag on the passenger seat. I quickly jumped over or wall round the garden and ran to get my dad. He had seen the event and came running to meet me. The car drove away thankfully. At that time there were little kids being grabbed by men and being killed. The thought even today scares me.

A year or so later I was in Easdale, that quiet wee highland place where everyone knows everyone. I was walking with my cousin Agnes along the road to the only shop to get some shopping for my aunt. A car stopped and offered a lift to us. I refused to get in the car. It was a very elderly couple who my cousin knew. I was adamant that there was no way I was getting into the car, and we walked the rest of the way. At home Agnes told her mum what had happened, and I got roasted from her for being so rude to the old folk. Eventually my dad got to hear the story and tried to explain to my aunt why I behaved in such a way. My aunt never said a word to me; I thought she should have apologised.

Then there was the weed killer disaster. Dad would plant nasturtiums every year around the garden. They grew happily from seed even with the soot and smoke of the city. On the other side would be antirrhinums or snapdragons--all very pretty, when in bloom. He had a patch of grass to cut and found it so hard to use the lawnmower, so I would help with the gardening. We were working away, weeding grass, cutting, and tidying up when dad asked me to go and put two capfuls of feed into the watering can and fill it with water. Instead of feed I mistakenly put in weed killer. It was awful, and I was so upset at my stupidity. My mum was out watering all the flowers afterwards, and most of them died. On saying that the nasturtiums survived as always, every year an orange walk went by our house. They marched down

Gower Street, playing flutes, brass instruments, drums, and anything that made a racket. It was serious stuff.

My family would get four chairs out and sit in the garden waving to the marchers, all of them dressed as though going to a wedding, they would wave back to us. We never had a drop of litter in our garden as the orange flowers were treated with respect. Every other garden had litter everywhere in it though.

My dad was born 12th of July, Orange Walk Day. He was asked to become leader of the Glasgow branch but declined. He felt it annoyed the Catholic people around us, and so never joined their happy band. They told him how silly he was turning it down, as he would have been the top man in the march carrying a velvet cushion with important regalia on it, but he still said no thanks.

Easdale had a lot of funny stories from my dad. He had a good memory for hilarious things happening on the island, and one of his classic ones was the cat story. There were two very old brothers that had a cottage on Easdale before the war. They were both in their 90s and had stayed there all their lives. They had a pet cat "Jock", as old has themselves in cat years. Jock was often unwell and had stomach troubles. One week he was so bad being sick and diarrhea around the place, so the kindest thing for the old men to do was put him to sleep. A great discussion happened to decide the kindest way to do this awful thing, and finally they thought it best to take Jock to the local quarry and send him to heaven.

Jock was carried carefully along the narrow path leading to the quarry, the old men stood at the water's edge and said a prayer for Jock's happy life on Easdale. Then with great sadness he was gently put into a cloth bag with a stone to weigh him down and it was tied at the top after which he was flung into the very deep dark quarry. Down sank Jock into the black water the same depth as the height of Ben Nevis, and the old men felt heart broken, tears streamed down their wrinkled cheeks, and out came the white handkerchiefs as they walked slowly home.

On arriving at their cottage as they walked into the small sitting room, low and behold here was Jock sitting soaking wet in an armchair by the fire, licking his furry coat dry and looking very pleased with himself. Jock's time was not up yet, and he lived on after a recovery from his sickness. He surely had 9 lives.

Another story was of Hughy the local man who had just got married at 50yrs and was asked how married life was. His answer was, "Well, she's not very beautiful, but she's economical." This comment caused great hilarity in the pub that night. Hughy's classic tale was the Gaelic story.

Hughy thought himself an expert in the Gaelic language repeating words in what was his native tongue. One night my uncle took a tape recorder to the pub and switched it on asking Hughy to sing a Gaelic song for all the drinkers. Hughy being the biggest show off began to sing with baritone sounds a well-known song in Gaelic. There was a huge clap from the listeners when he finished, and my uncle took his tape home and the family listened to Hughy again singing his heart out.

Some weeks later my uncle took the tape recorder to the pub and asked Hughy for his opinion on this wonderful Gaelic singer (unknown to Hughy it was himself). The pub listened transfixed, my uncle said, "Well, Hughy what do you think of that eh?" Hughy answered, "Well he's a brilliant singer, but his Gaelic's hellish," at that the pub drinkers had such a laugh.

Hughy never found out the name of the singer, and just as well it would have burst his bubble.

Holidays were such fun in Easdale and I was always sad to leave, back in Glasgow it was still school holidays and we played out the back green. The only other nasty experience I had in our back green was when some old guy came and flashed his crown jewels at me. At that I heard a scream from above, and a woman on the top floor house next close had seen him also. She flung a pot out the window to scare him and told me to run inside and lock the back gate. I escaped the crazy man. Turned out a few years ago (2018), I was getting a new kitchen at my house in Aberdeen. The joiner who fitted it stayed next close to me, and his mum was the lady with the pot. Small world.

The back green was used for women washing clothes in the small boiler houses. They all took their turns in a washing day, and the boiler had to be lit at 4am so that it would have plenty of hot water. That all stopped when there were steamies or washing machines. Outside we played all day until dark and the light went on in the street.

Boys played football, kick the can, or just chase the girls. The girls played skipping, balls against the walls, peever, dolls, schools, and made tents with blankets and brushes. Endless fun and never ever bored. The rainy days were also fun, and games in the close too.

We wore shorts and t-shirts in summer, my dad picked out our clothes. He thought we looked smart, and I thought we looked like boys and hated the look, but we had no say. Every other girl had on a summer dress with hair ribbons, and the only dress I had was for church and that was only worn on Sundays. My Mum would lock us out because otherwise Anna and I were in and out all day. We were only allowed in for meals, a drink of water, or the toilet. At that young age I didn't know anything else and accepted everything as the right way.

My poor wee mum had terrible depression on and off, and I sometimes wonder if she was homesick for Oban. The difference between Oban and Glasgow was vast. Dad would take her to the doctors and most times she would be admitted to Leverndale Mental Hospital which was not a cheery place to go if you were depressed. I worked there as a student nurse, and it was enough to make a sane person mental. Once she was there it was a short stay ward, Anna and I would go and visit her. We were very young and really it was not a safe place to walk around, one day the ward sister took us both into her office we thought we had done something wrong, she said, "Girls, just let me say how much I admire you both for visiting your mum, nobody else gets visitors here". I thought it nice of her to say that.

We brought sweets, soap, clean clothes, and other things that helped mum feel better, we never had much to talk about and neither did she, it was heartbreaking to leave after the visit and see her in such a sad place.

Modern medicine helped later, and she had a new lease of life in her old age, playing bingo, chatting to neighbours, fish and chip nights, and bus trips paid for by the council. One Christmas time I phoned her from Aberdeen to see when I could visit her in her sheltered housing, "Wait till I see my diary," she said, "I have 17 meals to go to, I'm a Muslim on Saturday for a meal at the Mosque, I'm a Jewish person on

15

Monday for a meal at the Synagogue", and on she went, happy as a sand woman enjoying her old age.

One day I got a phone call that she had collapsed and died of a massive heart attack. She was 76, a bit overweight but loved life in the end. A post-mortem was carried out as she died at home. Anna phoned to see if she could view the body, and the Mortician said it would cost £40 to "tidy her up" before viewing. I said, "Anna, just remember her as she was, don't go there," she didn't and mum was buried in Easdale, Balvicar Cemetery. We stood like covenanters around her grave. Everyone there loved her dearly. Anna and I arranged to have a photo of my parents on their tombstone, and it's still there today after so many years. Today Anna lies beside them.

Chapter 2

Bellahouston
Parish Church

Happy Days of Sunshine

Summers were endless, warm, and sunny. I remember that most years we all went to Easdale to see my dad's family, there were plenty of cousins, uncles, and aunts, even neighbours were part of our holiday fun, I loved Easdale with its wide shores and crashing Atlantic waves, the strong smell of the sea, wildflowers, sheep and fields of barley and wheat, all such a great experience compared to the hot city of Glasgow in summer. There was always the smell of beer, sickness, smoke, dust, and bad drains in the city.

Litter was everywhere, and people didn't wash much then so human smells were always part of life. To travel on a bus, I would jump on and walk to the end of the seats, sniffing as I walked, then would sit on the least smelly seat. Old women were the worst, and they sat with their legs open, and the stink of urine knocked out everyone around them. This sounds very snobbish, which I am not, but soap and water don't cost a lot so there was no excuse for it.

Easdale was a complete release from this horror, and all my family would travel to the back of the island and have a huge sausage picnic, rolls in butter, brown and tomato sauce all cooked in a frying pan made of wood gathered by the children. We must have looked like tinks or gypsies gathering on the slates.

Back at my school after the holidays the teacher would ask the class where they went. I was only one of two kids who put their hand up. I never realised that nobody went on holiday back then, and we got a free board with my aunt. My dad I'm sure would give her something to help with the food bill, but that was it- "Highland Hospitality".

Visiting relatives was very important to dad. We would travel on a bus to East Kilbride, or train to Dumbarton. We enjoyed seeing our cousins, aunts, and uncles. Easdale would be the main topic of conversation. One day it was the Glasgow Fair, and every Glaswegian got their two weeks pay before the fortnight holiday. Train stations were packed with travelers sitting on suitcases waiting for trains. A lot of them went to Saltcoats, Ayr or Largs. All these places made a fortune with the Glasgow people, and they spent every penny of their pay on hotel, food, and in the local shops.

Dad decided that it would be nice to visit my Aunt Anna and her family in Dumbarton several miles out of Glasgow, so we all set off for the trip on the train. As we came out of Dumbarton Train Station we walked through a park, and my sister and I always walked behind my parents. My foot kicked something on the path, and I turned to see what it was, and here was a wallet. It was Dad's, and he looked so shocked when I ran up to him with my lucky find.

Inside the Wallet was his two weeks' pay and some extra savings for our holiday. I was the hero of the day, and Dad was so relieved that he never lost it, and he told us our holiday would have been disastrous if the wallet was lost. I think it was the only money in the world he had. Another happy ending.

There was another lucky find of money for me when I was about 9 years old. Again, another Glasgow Fair Story. We were making plans to visit Easdale for the two weeks holiday, and this meant Anna and I would need swimsuits and new underwear, so off we all walked the mile journey to Woolworths at Paisley Road Toll. It was not a pleasant journey, with lots of traffic on Paisley Road, pubs stinking of booze and sickness on every corner. Dog's dirt everywhere (no picking up dog poo then) and there were always tough looking men drunk as monkeys walking past us or looking for money.

It was a relief to get into the fabulous shop that every Glaswegian loved, Woolworths. It fascinated me when I was young, as you could purchase just about everything you needed in life to be happy, and at that time everything was only sixpence. There were biscuits, chocolate, cream, sugar, everything you could buy, even broken biscuits were a great hit as they sold for a song. Underwear was for all sizes, men's, children's, and ladies. Even a paint counter with all sorts of colours. I loved it.

We all strolled in, my Dad always the joker with us would put on a very upper-class accent, at that all the folk who heard him would turn in horror that a posh person had the cheek to enter their favourite store. We all would have a laugh at the looks he got from the Glaswegians. It's a wonder he never got punched, as then the upper classes were despised.

We went to look at the bag and purse counter. As a child I was not allowed to touch anything in a shop unless told by my parents. This time, however, I noticed a very shabby looking purse among all the brand-new ones. I picked it up and gave it to Dad, and he told the assistant about the find. He suggested he gave it to the manager, and the assistant suggested the local police station would be better. So off we set up the road to the police station, and on the way Dad and Mum went into a close and counted the contents of the purse. It was £25, a fortune then, that was more than two weeks of my Dad's wages.

The policeman took the purse and took our name and address. A day later there was a ring at our door, it was a policeman, he had said that the purse was claimed and handed over £2.6s in reward. I was so please to get this money as my name was on the reward. I went to put it in my desk where I kept my meagre savings, and Dad suggested seeing it was so much that he would take care of it and buy me something with it. He bought two summer dresses for my sister and I. They were his choice of colours. I was a bit miffed that I hadn't kept my treasure, but he showed me not to be selfish, which young children are sometimes.

When the weather was warm my Dad would decorate a room, and this was a huge undertaking. The paint stank and took ages to dry, and colours were few. Wallpaper was the ghastliest patterns, huge flowers mostly. Dad chose the living room paper, and it was squares of different browns, reminded him of wood samples he said, then for the final flourish he chose three different coloured curtains: pale green, orange, and turquoise. The neighbours must have thought we were all nuts, but he thought the whole wonderful colour scheme looked beautiful and would sit and admire his design project. Even the ornaments were his choice.

I think my mum just left him to it and, she maybe thought, "Well he has been a POW for so long he could now have some enjoyment." We had a huge porcelain salmon staring back at us from the display shelf, and then a huge eagle with giant wingspan taking up one shelf. Dad wanted The Monarch of the Glen (a Stag). Thankfully that never came to fruition, and he ran out of money (thank goodness).

We helped paper the walls, and I was about 12 years old at this time. My job was to make a small tear at the bottom of each roll as dad held the paper at the top of the ladder--it was a great height with high ceilings. Once or twice I got it wrong then he had to patch the bottom with much moaning about waste. I then had to put the paste on with a brush careful not to miss any bits, all this was done with army precision even when he cut the paper with the breadknife. One time the paper didn't stick too well, and a couple of sheets rolled down the wall it was like the end of the world. I had to reassure him that it was never a problem and we could just stick it back up, I always was a problem solver with a happy way of doing things he said.

Some work in the house could not be done by dad, like plumbing, that was serious stuff and not to be treated lightly, so money was saved each week (never credit cards then) you bought with cash or did without. Dad decided we needed a new bathroom suite, so it was New Year and the plumber appeared after the holidays, an elderly man with his bag of tools and pipes to be fitted, Mum being mum and kind as always, offered the man a sherry to toast in the New Year (neither of my parents were drinkers). It was from the one and only bottle of sherry.

The old pull chain toilet was removed, a nice new white bath with no rust stains fitted, and posh looking washbasin installed. That afternoon I came home from school to see this fabulous new loo. I sat down to wee and found I was facing to the left of the normal position. I finished and then shouted on dad to see that the toilet was fitted squint. He then quizzed my mum; she told him about the "little sherry". He looked at the bottle it was half empty, the plumber had been drunk, he was called back to fix it, and all was forgiven.

Every Sunday there was church, and everything was prepared the night before. Shoes were polished, clothes laid out, clean handkerchiefs, sweets, not to be touched until told, bibles, and hymn books. We had baths Saturday night to smell good and look clean for God.

The carillon bells rang out at 10.30 am waking every heathen in the vicinity. We all walked the short distance to Bellahouston Parish Church at the top of the road. Inside it was quiet with the smell of moth balls everywhere. I had a card that was stamped when I attended (regularly every week).

The minister was very serious looking standing in the pulpit. He spoke quietly, but if he noticed anyone nodding off, he would shout and bawl like a madman and we all jumped with fright. It was fire and brimstone stuff he spoke of. He would say hell was real and avoid it at all costs. At the start of the 45 min sermon, dad reached into the sweet bag and passed Anna and I a treacle caramel, the size of an old penny. Our lips were sealed, and you could not talk with this huge sweet in your mouth and it stuck to your teeth, gums, and top pallet of your mouth.

I would sit and look at the beautiful stained-glass windows, pictures of Jesus with sheep, Moses, the disciples, all fascinated me at that young age. The only scary thing I would see which creeped me out was the old lady in front with a dead fox around her neck. Its eyes stared back at me, and I never thought for a moment it was real. I thought someone made them to look that way. Communion was a very serious event. I always think God has a great sense of humour. Wine for blood, bread for body, my parents participated in this, only snag, it was large silver cups filled with red wine, they were passed along the rows of the congregation and not even wiped after each person. We had a Sunday school teacher with buck teeth and he slobbered a lot too. Nobody sat next to the poor man at communion.

The one service I did listen to with intent was when the minister read from the book of Corinthians chapter 1, verse 13. This hit home to me and made me quite emotional. Even at 10 years old, the minister's voice, the church atmosphere all contributed to my tears running down my cheeks, it was a special moment and I am grateful to mum and dad for showing me the right way in my life.

Once as a teenager I got a new pair of stockings with hold up suspenders belt, I had put the belt on the wrong way round, meaning that there were two suspenders digging into the back of my legs, consequently I sat on the church's hard wooden pew in agony for two solid hours. I can still feel the pain writing this, I was so glad to get home.

My sister was three years younger and to my horror she got the same outfit two weeks after me. Mum said she was my height so should wear them (she was only 12 years old). One day my friend and I were watching her cross the road to the shops, and there was a young lad behind her. The stockings and suspenders both fell to her ankles, and the confused guy couldn't stop staring at the apparition in front of him. We laughed so much at her embarrassment as kids do.

I wore diamond mesh, and thought them so trendy, tights only came out when miniskirts were in fashion. I do recall having only one jumper at school. Things were very tight with money when my parents were unwell. Dad would be taken to hospital one month, mum taken the next month. That's just how it always was. Very difficult for both, but they tried so hard to keep things running smoothly to their credit.

Illness was just God's way of teaching us to be humble and grateful for small things. Eight pounds a week was the sick pay, and not enough for a growing family. They were genuinely sick too, which made things worse. The lack of money made worries magnify and did no good for their health.

Gran came to stay at Clifford Street for a couple of years. She and mum never got on, which is normal. It helped when illness struck either parent to have her around. I loved her to bits and she could do no wrong in my eye. My sister did not get on with her and gave her a hard time, "I was the pet", she said. Gran would have me read her the Bible each night. Anna was not allowed in the room--she was maybe too young--but gran would chase her away.

One morning gran made her usual huge pot of porridge, enough to feed an army. Anna sat at the table with a massive portion in front of her, and she refused to touch it. To my horror, gran ran after her with a wooden spoon, and Anna ended up locking herself in the bathroom until my mum came home from work. Mum took Anna's side of the story, and shortly after that gran went to stay in Edinburgh with my Aunt Jenny.

When I was 12 years old, I had my appendix out. Dr. Russell came to my house and said, "That I had to get to the hospital with my abdominal pain immediately or I could die." This put my poor parents in a flap, but they were allowed to escort me to the hospital (they would not be allowed in the ambulance today). I got there and was prepared for theatre. I recall dad giving me a kiss as though it was my last, but the operation went well and I recovered with only pain from the prodding in my tummy.

I was in a ward with elderly ladies who all had huge medical problems. The end bed where very sick were put seemed to empty often. One minute I would hear someone's death rattle (breathing before death) and the next they would disappear. I had the bright idea to put a sheet over my head to avoid seeing any more trauma. The nurse got annoyed with me for doing this, I suppose I looked like a corpse, but being young I thought this was great to bloke out all going on around me.

Mum sent me back to school after two weeks, I was still in pain and stiff to walk, one day in class a boy pushed me and I yelled in agony. The tough guy of the class said, "Leave her alone, anyone touch her and they are done for". This surprised me as he was a real bad rascal and the whole class was scared stiff from him. He left School at 15 and went on to murder his uncle and cousin, mutilating her body afterwards. I often wonder how a young boy could be so cruel yet he showed compassion for me after my operation. Years later I read a book "The Real

Taggarts" there on a page was the story of my classmate. It was known as the Kinning Park Murder. The girl he killed was deaf and dumb, he mutilated her small body. He also killed his uncle doing the same to him. They caught him with a bloody toe print on the floor. I was so shocked to think that I used to sit next to him in class.

My other hospital trip was for a broken collar bone. I had been out with friends and two boys held me at each end and swung me. I landed with a thud and broken bone, and a week later Dad thought I had a slope in my shoulder. I told him it was sore, and when I got to the ER room they said it was a break in my collar bone shown on the x-ray. I had a strapping tied over my shoulder area. My pal's surname was Broadfoot. I was christened Broadshoulder-- always the Comics in Glasgow even in times of pain.

Mary Broadfoot was such a good friend, and we would walk for miles together, share stories of our family's ill health, and go swimming every Saturday morning at Summerton Road Baths with nobody but us in the Pool. We would walk home have lunch and then meet up to walk down to the Finniston Ferry which was free. It took you over the River Clyde to the West end of Glasgow, a short walk to Kelvingrove Art Galleries for some culture, no wonder I was skinny.

Another of Mary and my bright ideas was to go to Judo Classes. Mary was two heads taller than I, so we both enrolled in a class at night in the school. Here we thought we would learn how to defend ourselves from the wild men of Glasgow. The learning of throws was going well, me a smurf-sized girl, my partner Mary built with strong bones and much taller than I, and athletic appearance, we were to practice a throw on each other, she threw me first, I landed on the mat in true judo fall. Mary looking chuffed that she managed this difficult manoeuvre. Then it was my turn, before Mary had time to think I grabbed her shoulder swung round and at that she fell on the floor. I was delighted to be able to do this to someone taller than me, until in horror I discovered she landed wrong and had broken her thumb. The two of us ended up going home. Mary got a plaster stooky on her thumb up to her elbow. I felt so bad and apologised profusely to her.

The next day in class everyone cheered as I walked in (Glasgow people love a story about a fight). The English Teacher pretended to hide under the table from me, poor Mary sat in pain, and I felt no hero.

My other friend who at first I only saw on Sundays at choir practice or Sunday school was Ann Miller (I'm still in touch with her after all those years). She came to Glasgow at 7 years old, and she and I were complete opposites. Ann had a brain like a sponge, mine was more like mince then. She was always top of the class competing with Ian MacBeth (another brainy kid). We all clapped when Ann got top place and it became a weekly entertainment that all we dull heads enjoyed.

Ann also went swimming with me in Bellahouston Baths across the road. On the first visit I asked Mum for a shilling and sixpence for entry and sixpence for a bag of chips after the swim. Mum asked if I could swim (she knew I couldn't). Well, her grand piece of advice for swimming was, "Just don't go deeper than your waist, stand a bit away from the pole at the edge and practice swimming towards it."

Off I went to the pool, and while trying out my Mum's wonderful swimming advice I found sure enough I could swim. I discovered Ann and I were the only girls there, and we changed in the only cubicle, each taking turns to hold the door closed. It was one of these crazy designs where you could see your head and your feet, anyway into the pool we went, Ann Swimming away, me practicing my strokes. It came easily to me, and I was swimming within a few minutes.

After much practice I could swim like a fish darting here and there avoiding the amorous males our same age. We played with a beach ball in two teams racing after it with strong strokes. We swam for ages like a pair of dolphins. After our swim in was the showers with pink carbolic soap. I loved it and felt clean as a whistle after my scrub. Until on occasion a couple of boys would grab hold of us and fling us in the pool again. Ann and I got fly to this and went to the showers 15 minutes before the boys--sorted.

Years later at nursing college, I beat the record for breaststroke, and was entered for the Glasgow College competition in swimming. I was up against tall athletic girls. Folk shouted, "Come on Twiggy", as I swam for my life in the pool. I came in third after a lane of breaststroke, one of Crawl, lastly Butterfly. I suppose I could have done better but shyness gave me more butterflies than the swimming stroke.

Ann studied Astronomy at Glasgow University. I was to accompany her on many trips to observatories viewing the stars and planets, and this I loved and was also so interested in the subject. I learned a lot from these visits. We were also great Sunday school pals, and both of us went on to Bible class later. I didn't stay long at that, and it sounded too argumentative for my liking.

Years later Ann and husband Richard invited me to their beautiful house in France, set beside a River and Mill, with walks along its edges for miles. They got this house so that it was easy for cycling along. I didn't speak a word of French and felt an idiot when Ann's French friends came over, just smiling at them and nodding my head as though I knew what they were saying, like one of those nodding dogs at the back of a car. So I decided to try my luck in learning French (they say learning a language when old helps prevent Alzheimer's Disease, I felt it brought it on) anyway one day I went out on my own for a river walk. As I trotted along I saw three young women approach me. I thought I'll try some of my French words, so as they passed I said, "Bonjour." One of them turned and said to me, "Are you from Glasgow?" I replied yes in amazement. She was from Edinburgh and recognised my accent. So much for me trying to sound French.

CHAPTER 3

"The Queen".

Learning about life and how to behave.

School, well some love it, some hate it, I felt a bit of both, primary was fine, I loved reading, learning about things in life, and the teachers were nice gentle souls, never a harsh word from them, angels in grey suits I thought. In those days some wore their graduation gowns to keep the chalk of their clothes. One teacher wore a tight grey suit, with a bright pink hat perched on her head. Mrs. Mac, she would be about 60 years old and about to retire.

Her daughter was also a teacher in the same school, Bellahouston Infants. Mrs. Mac hated rubbers, erasers if you are American. This my dad did not know. He bought me a brand-new rubber for school and I was warned to guard this rubber with my life. I was 7 years old and it cost a lot and was to be taken care of. I was writing away happily in my very best writing (second best writer in class) when I made a mistake, I looked up to see if Mrs. Mac was looking my way, great she was filing her nails, so out comes the new Rubber, then a voice from across the passage shouts, "Please Miss Iona MacQueen is using a RUBBER," horror of horrors, a huge gasp came from all the class. One boy shouted "Grass" a term used in Glasgow for someone who tells on others. I was asked to come to front of class. My heart pounded, sweat was on my back, my legs shook with fear.

Was it the belt? Was I expelled? Was I suspended? Was it a letter to my parents? All this jumbled around my wee head. It's great how adults put the fear of death in kids. "Hand it over," I heard, "What Miss?", I said. "You know what, pass it over to me." Time to tell porky pies I quickly thought. "Empty your pockets," she said, so I did. Mum would give me my play piece in mother's pride wrapping paper, so out on the table I extracted from my pockets six mother's pride wrappings. The class erupted in hoots of laughter. The teacher asked, "Why carry all this rubbish around in your pockets?" I replied, "Because my folks said it's wrong to drop litter." This caused more hilarious laughing, the class by now was out of control, and still no sign of the rubber. A voice shouted from the front, "It's in her hand Miss." More sweat, palpitations, and tremors. I was thinking of my dad's face when I told him, "Oh, I've lost the rubber, please God don't let this happen to me." Then I meanly handed it to her after 15 mins of searching. She threw it into the empty dark green bin-- "Go back to your seat now." As the class finished, Mrs. Mac said to me when all had left, "Take your rubber out of the bin and never tell lies again, you will remember this all your life." She was right and I've never forgotten the feeling even to this day at 71 years old.

We had to curtsy if we were girls and the boys saluted when our teacher walked into the playground in the morning. It was like the Queen arriving I thought, but it was her way of demanding respect. I did like her a lot though and learned how to write in calligraphy which is admired by all even today. Mrs. Mac could have taught today's teachers how important how we write is, then if you applied for a job, it was a written letter, so a lot could be said about a person's character by their writing.

I recall when my two sons were at school in Aberdeenshire. I looked at their homework and saw these dreadful scrawls over the paper. I went to the school to suggest they give the boys some writing tuition. The headmistress was appalled at my idea. "We don't care how the writing looks Mrs. McLean, it's the content." I could not believe what I was hearing. I taught them at home myself how to write legibly. How times have changed.

After infant's school came primary. Ibrox Primary was a Victorian building across from Ibrox Park. There I had good and bad teachers, and the classes were a large mix of boys and girls, with both words written in red stone above each playground. We were separated from the boys while playing. The boys were from another planet with wildness, shouting, fighting, kicking and anything else that abhorred us. Sometimes you would go up to the fence to look in at them and a face would appear with mucous runny nose, a swear word would come out of his mouth or a sly grin to scare us, and we ran away in fear. We girls were more creative with skipping ropes, balls, and other games, sometimes just chatting quietly to each other.

We had a teacher who combed her hair in a small mirror propped up on the window. She could see us all in the reflection. She had beautiful wavy jet black hair and wore a turquoise overall. I liked her a lot. She left to have a baby which I never understood and why leave for that?

Another teacher also wore overalls. She was tall and very skinny, and she would leap up the stairs two at a time like a Jenny long legs. She wore soft dark blue slippers, so this allowed her to jump on each step. Her hair was like a Brillo pad parted in the middle, Kirby grips to hold it back on each side. Most days she was out of class chatting to the teacher next door, and the kids then made such a racket you couldn't hear yourself think. The school had huge light blue railings with sharp tops, probably to keep us in. We got a mix of subjects. Geography I loved. History was a bit scary, but worth hearing about. One teacher read from a book for each English lesson. I thought this was great and listened to every word she said.

Sums and mental arithmetic were never my forte. I was terrified when the teacher shouted my name to answer a sum in my head. I think it terrified me for life about counting, even when older I always got my arithmetic checked by another although I could do it ok, but I never had the confidence to count.

Every Tuesday night I went to the Red Cross. Their motto for emergency situations was "Always Stay Cool, Calm, and Collected." I wanted even at 12 to be a Nurse, so why not start there? I gained many badges but was quite unruly in class. I loved to chat to my pal and giggle when asked about stools, thinking they were wooden pieces of furniture, then discovering they were faeces. An elderly lady who taught us, gave up her Tuesday nights to be with us. One night an older student took me aside and told me off for chatting in class. She was right to do this, after that I behaved. I think I loved fun and laughter, jokes and carry on, and I didn't see the bigger picture, I'm sure a lot of kids are like me today, that's why they don't learn, their heads are full of nonsense like mine was.

After Red Cross my pal and I went over to see if there were any casualties at the Rangers match. You got in free the last half hour, so there we were in uniform looking for some unfortunate soul, back then it was safe for us, as most of the men were parents themselves. There were the odd drunks, but we were there to save lives ages 12. I always wondered why a lot of the men stood facing the walls at the back. I thought they were praying for their team, and when I discovered they were urinating I never went back.

Part of our Red Cross learning was entering competitions with other Red Cross groups. This meant going to Maryhill Red Cross Centre, with groups from all over Glasgow. It was a big hall with seats for the parents and spectators. There were six juniors in my group, and we waited outside until called to perform on a stage. It was quite nerve wracking for kids my age, but a learning curve. We all ran into the hall, and there was a loud clap from the audience which made our nerves worse. There on stage was an older kid lying pretending to be unconscious. Quickly we all looked around for the cause of this drama. I spotted an electric plug with a black stain around it. Now was our time to shine. I picked up a wooden spoon on the table and swiped off the electric, then we put the poor casualty into the unconscious position, and he came around and said he felt fine.

At that, one of the rescuers trapped the rug from the floor and began to fan him with it. The audience were in hysterics at this point, and the scene turned into a comedy. Someone tripped over the rug and fell with a glass of water in their hand. The patient was soaked. I don't recall the outcome, but we sure gave the audience a good laugh. My Dad had taught me never to touch electric when it's on unless it's with something wooden. I suppose if had been real we could all have been blown up.

Chapter 4

Mr. Jinks.

When I was about 8 years old, we got a dog. He was one of a litter of six and the only Survivor. Half Corgi and half Cairn, a Royal mum and a rag tag Dad. He was free, and in those days most dogs didn't cost money. He had a license, a collar, and his name tag with a lead. Dad said he looked like a rat when a pup, and we loved him as a brother. He was given the usual vaccinations dogs got, and his mother's milk had dried up so at six weeks old he arrived at our house in a cardboard box with cozy blanket, needing lactose milk to survive which he did with great gusto. Jinks lived 20 until years old, which is very old indeed for a dog.

When weaned from milk he got a bowl of porridge for breakfast and a small tin of Kenomeat dog food for supper, and nothing else. My mother knew about dogs, her father being a farmer and dog trainer. She didn't allow us to feed him between meals-- no treats, no nibbles from the table. It did him no harm and I'm sure contributed to his longevity.

I came home from school at lunch and took him out for a walk, when home later I would walk him for hours on end round parks and streets in the area. Everyone knew Jinks, and you could be out for a walk and a complete stranger would say hello to him.

When he was a pup, Anna and I took him to the park. She was young at the time and somehow, he escaped from her when holding the lead. He ran on to Paisley Road, full of buses and traffic and was hit by a bus. She carried him home in her arms crying all the way. We put him on a double bed in the kitchen. My mum examined him and said, "Well girls, I don't think he has broken any bones, it's just bruising." How she could come away with this diagnosis beats me. He survived, but always ran with his hind legs at a slight twist. He probably had a broken pelvis to, but he was a tough wee dog and never bothered a sniff. Vets were for the rich, so he never saw one all his life until the end.

One day I took him up the street for a walk, and a young lad was walking towards me with a white poodle on a lead. Jinks made a jump at the dog, mounted her, and started to enjoy himself. I was mortified, and the guy shouted at me to get my f...... dog off her. It took some time and much pulling on Jinks lead, and the whole event left me shaken and upset. Jinks had a very high sex drive and I mean very high. One time a friend asked me to keep Jinks away from his cat for the previous reasons. Another time the lady upstairs had a pup that was in heat. Well Jinks went mental at not getting out to perform. He sat in the kitchen and howled most of the day.

Dad had been ill in bed with his heart condition looking blue in colour. Jinks was making him worse, so in his wisdom and unknown to us he gave Jinks two Mogadon sleeping tablets for humans. I came home and Jinks was sleeping like a log. This sleep lasted two whole days, Jinks with shallow breathing not stirring even for food, we thought he was dying. The next-door neighbour came in to visit Dad when ill and saw the dog and came to the conclusion that he had banged his head on a goal post across at the pitches. Dad never told us the true reason for the great sleep until he woke up, and we were all horrified that Jinks could have gone to heaven.

On occasions when the front door was opened Jinks made a dart for freedom, and off he would run hiding from his captors out into the wild west of Glasgow. We would run after him, but he was fast as a whippet, and he was also fly as a fox and would hide from us when searching. It was often the police station where he ended up, and there he sat with the station sergeant drinking tea with his nose deep inside a mug. Sometimes he would end up at the cat and dog home, where for seven pounds he got out. Dad went nuts if it was there, the threat was if it happened again then no way was he coming home, but always he did.

One time he disappeared for a week. Searches by all the kids in the area began, and nobody had seen him, until a knock at the door came a woman with news of his whereabouts. He was at the dog woman's house--some wifey who took in stray dogs. Jinks wasn't stray, and he had his name tag on. Anyway, Dad gave her money for his week of food and home he came.

I was dating at the time and my boyfriend would sleep in the living room in a sleeping bag. He discovered a terrible itch everywhere with spots. Jinks had caught fleas, there were no flea collars then and if there were we never heard of them. Everyone in my class at school was scratching, and my boyfriend wore a white coat at work and a flea was seen jumping over it. Dad was horrified, "I expected this in the German prisoner of war camp, but not my home." He said Jinks was not the dog of the moment.

Dad sent me to the chemists for treatment, and they gave me DDT, now banned as toxic. We poured it everywhere: beds, carpets, blankets, curtains--you name it. We then hoovered every corner of the house, and the last thing was Jinks. We took him to the bath and he was black with fleas. They had all jumped on him for escape from the DDT, and he was emersed in warm water until they all drowned. Then we rinsed him and gave him a haircut, which was one of my specialties.

After that we never saw another Flea, but after that Jinks had a weekly bath in case they returned. We would say, "Jinks time for a bath" and he would dart under the bed, a long brush was the only way to catch him. He hated all that washing, we even started to spell the word BATH but he then knew exactly what it meant. As I sit and write this I am scratching at the memory.

One time he escaped from the house and I saw him in a pram with about six kids pushing it. He had his front paws boldly on the hood like king of the castle tearing down a hill at top speed.

He could sense your every mood and would lick our hand it you were upset. He was more human than dog, and he would wait for the cross now sign on the traffic lights before going over the busy road.

When just a pup we took him to Newcastle to visit my Aunt Joan and Uncle Ernest. They had two teenaged sons much older than Anna and I. Uncle Ernest made Jinks a cardboard box for a bed it was lined with foam for comfort with his name in bold letters on top, we thought this great. When we came down for breakfast in the morning there was a great to do with the adults, much apologising was heard from my parents, Jinks had eaten all the foam and had sickness and diarrhea all over the rooms, they left the doors open over the house so as to hear the dog if he needed out, Jinks being in a strange house didn't bark for to go out, so the end result was spew and whoopsie everywhere.

Another time while on a train journey Jinks was put into a big bag, my dad's idea on avoiding the 9 pound cost for a dog on the train. Anna and I were to carry the bag a handle each. As we went through the ticket gate, a black nose appeared to the ticket collector. He didn't comment and probably knew why a dog was in a bag.

After the Newcastle holiday, dad came home and made Jinks a wooden bed, it was a masterpiece, painted with pale green paint, a pillow to lie on, and his name painted on the front. It lasted all his long life.

Jinks was always fit as a fiddle, he could run and walk for miles, and outrun any dog around. I was nursing when years later Anna phoned to tell me Jinks was very ill. She was going to the vets and thought it was the end for him. I was working in a busy surgical ward at the time and no way would I be able to come with her. It was one of those decisions you make in life and regret. I never went with her, and she had the hard task of agreeing to the vet that Jinks was ready for heaven.

It was so sad to hear of his leaving us, but he had such a great wee life. He was loved by so many people, even my cousins, when a record called, "Hot Dog Buddy Buddy" was played, Jinks would go nuts. My cousins laughed so much at this performance, and the song reminds me always of a great wee dog.

CHAPTER 5

Nurses Uniform.

Education

Secondary School was a disaster for me. It was a new comprehensive school at the top of Gower Street with lots of glass windows and venetian blinds. It was filled with hopeless teachers with no clue how to control teenagers, with the results that most of the kids were idiots including myself then.

With no guidance for life's journey, advice on how to succeed, or interest in their pupils, it accommodated 1,300 Pupils from surrounding areas all put into classes according to their brain ability, or so they thought. It turned out I was in the wildest class in the school with a mix of males and females every one of us thought to be daft as brushes and not worth the bother teaching. One History teacher as much as told us all on our first day, that none of us would do anything other than work in a factory or become builders, "We were all complete idiots," were his words.

Another teacher would sit and talk about his life outside school, and another kept porn magazines in a drawer and asked my pal and I to tidy his drawers. Another liked to touch the girls inappropriately.

The gym teacher would walk over through where all of us had a shower and got changed, and he would just prance into the changing room a have a good look around. We were only 13 years old. One of the girls one day got us all to sit on a bench in turns placed over the door, and he ended up shouting like a maniac trying to enter, and he never did again.

There was only one great teacher: Mr. Norman McLeod from the Highlands. He taught us Geography and he also taught Gaelic. He was tall with red hair, handsome, and fit looking as they say today. The first day he taught us, one of the pupils started to act smart, chatting and joking. All of the class was terrified of this boy (the bad lad who ended up a murderer) and he ruled the roost. Mr. McLeod got him out of his seat and gave him six very hard smacks of the belt, and he was crying like a baby. The whole class was shocked, we all sat like quiet mice with not a word said for each lesson. I got 98% in Geography and my other classmates also did well.

If all the teachers had been like Mr. McLeod we would all have been geniuses, but sadly it wasn't to be. One teacher gave my pal and I lines for chatting as we came into class every day. I was asking her how her Dad was (he was dying of lung cancer) and she was asking be how my parents were (both of them were ill at the same time), but the lines kept me occupied every night for ages.

To top all the fear from the teachers there was the journey between every class to the next. I would sit in terror when the bell was rung as I knew I would be attacked, groped, and sexually assaulted by about six boys at a time. I thought it normal behaviour for boys to be like that, so never thought to tell my parents or teachers. I thought nobody would help, it was the most miserable feeling in the world at that time. I wasn't yet menstruating and had two pimples for breasts I was so skinny with not an ounce of fat on me.

Most children in my class had problems at home. Parents or siblings being ill, divorces happening, drunken fathers, neglectful mothers, lack of money for food, brothers beating them, all kinds of different problems. We were not idiots, but we were kids that never were encouraged to study, to learn, or to make a good life for ourselves. We didn't understand that if we had no thought for learning then we would never get a decent job ever.

The science class was where the porn teacher was. Strangely he kept us all quiet and listening, and one day he started to ask the class about the planet.

"What planet is nearest to the Sun?" I put my hand up and answered, "Mercury Sir,"

"That's right" he said.

"What Planet has rings round it?"

"Saturn," I answered. By this time the whole class was aghast at this spark of intelligence, "How do you know this he asked?"

"Well Sir, my dad bought me encyclopedic books so I read them every Sunday. The class erupted in laughter, so I never answered questions again. It was obvious that I was never going to succeed in this school, so thankfully my mum's cousin saved the day and suggested I went to nursing college where I would gain certificates to allow me to become a nurse, my dream job. Mind you, I thought it was just helping patients walk about and give them a glass of water when thirsty, never did I have a clue what the job entailed.

I wrote a Letter to Miss Winethorp to see if I could be accepted to enter this college in Bridgeton. My best writing came in handy and I was requested to come for an interview the following week, butterflies began the journey round my tummy from that moment, I could hardly sleep or think with the thought of what questions I would be asked, the day before the interview Dad asked me some questions that might come up. Why do you want to be nurse? Are any of your family nurses?

He was trying to make me feel confident for the following day. At last it came around, and my mother was to accompany me for the interview. Her Highland voice went down well with the three interviewers.

I was only 16 at the time, but understood that to get into the college was my only chance to start nursing. I was successful and delighted with my letter of acceptance. It was a two-year course, and we studied Anatomy, Physiology, and, Health, along with English and Science, and my least favourite subject Maths. After a year you concentrated on the subjects you were good at, and I was very lucky to gain the certificates needed for a hospital post.

We wore a uniform of blue dress with white starched collar, navy trench coat, and black sensible shoes. I recall going home on the bus with my pals. We had sat upstairs on the top deck, as we journeyed along the bus jilted to a stop with a thud, some boy had been knocked down. The next thing I heard was, "It's alright, there are three nurses upstairs. They will know what to do."

We looked at each other in horror. Surely, they don't mean us? Crumbs, neither of us have a clue. Panic struck us as we ran down the stairs like the guy in Dad's Army shouting "Don't Panic, Don't Panic" we have got this. Thankfully the poor boy was unhurt and shouted, "It's ok I'm fine" and he walked away, I don't know who was gladder, us or the bus driver.

My two pals were Roman Catholic. They went to Mass on Fridays, and I waited outside the church for them to complete their prayers. They were lovely girls, and we all got on so well even coming from different religions. By this time I was dating a boy who lived up the road from me, I would meet him at lunch time and we would go for a walk in Glasgow Green. The principal got to hear about this meeting and informed me that to be seeing a young man in uniform was most inappropriate. I told him this and he never saw me again.

We had to behave when outside, not that I did anything wrong, but it left things open to happen seeing a boy without a chaperone. We were given travel expenses for our journey to and from college. The bus collectors were always respectful to us. Most of them were Indian or Pakistani, and there was a shortage of bus drivers and conductors and a lot of Glaswegians did not want the job. In Glasgow it could be dangerous with drunks, guys with knives, tough gangs, and more so we were grateful for the new immigrants moving us around the city.

We had day visits to interesting places like the Southside Sewage Works. I nearly fell into the slurry pool on our day there, and we were all shocked at the sites we saw especially the wee man scraping sewage containing strange stuff not far from us, or the tractor lifting tons of the waste to another area. We had to be tough to see all that was happening and not be sick or faint.

Another trip was to Kingspark. This was to let us find out more about country life, fresh air, and flowers. As my colleagues walked on ahead of my Friends and I, they stopped to admire a huge Highland Bull. There were about ten girls standing chatting to him, and he turned around and sprayed them all with poo. Screams were heard and when we arrived we couldn't stop laughing at this scene, with all of them covered from top to toe in poo. One girl discovered we had missed it and was so annoyed at us for being untouched. The outing ended and we all had to go back home for a half day to clean up.

Miss MacDonald was our registration teacher, and she looked very severe. She had been a major during the war and nursed the pilots who came home burned and scarred from fighting. The stories she told us were heart rending, how they had turned from handsome young men into freaks with faces so awful that no woman would look at them. We thought of their plight and felt so sorry for them.

I learned a lot of Anatomy then and diseases with huge words like myxedema, comatose, rheumatoid arthritis. All these I knew the spelling of and remembered well. Once Miss MacDonald walked in with a huge bag, she set it down on the table and proceeded to take out five glass jars, each with a fetus at different stages of growth, we were all shocked at this site the first was an inch tall and the last like a premature baby all had been miscarried, it was a very moving lesson and one where I realised how precious life is.

We learned how to cook for the sick by making scrambled eggs, tripe, liver, bacon and more. I thought these foods would make me sicker, even sweetbreads were cooked these being brains and organs of animals. Today's vegans would have had a field day to hear of this lot, as they say in Glasgow, "Would gee you the Balk." I was sent to the local slaughterhouse with my pal to get a heart and some eyes for dissecting in biology, and it was something that was not pleasant to do but part of our learning.

Miss MacDonald disliked pubs and advised us all as young ladies to never enter them, never marry a man who drank, and to be wary of patients in future that smell of alcohol. She would chirp on for ages about the horrors of booze and I suppose it was good advice but scary to us.

Another piece of advice she gave us was that if we married then make sure you have your own bank book and savings account. I thought this would be a good idea if I ever got married, so announced this gem of wisdom to my dad. He was horrified and said, "When two people get married, then you have to trust each other." He wrote and complained to the college about the bad advice given to young girls. It was never mentioned who sent the letter to them, but I knew it was dad when Miss MacDonald mentioned girls speaking to their parents of her advice. Years later I realised it was particularly good advice indeed.

We went to the Citizen's Theatre for a show of *The Merchant of Venice*, which was so boring. I didn't understand a word spoken on the stage, and we had this as part of our English class. It all was so puzzling to a wee Scottish girl.

We had cooking lessons from a very young teacher, we had to make fruit salad. This entailed dissolving sugar, water, and lemon Juice over the heat. I put my solution on and it came to the boil, and I turned it down to simmer. At that the teacher shouted, "Right girls come round my desk please." This was for a tuition on the next stage of the fruit. At that the smell of burning emanated round the room, and I looked over at my pot cooking. It at been too high a heat and started to smoke.

I ran across put a damp cloth over it (my dad gave me lessons on how to put out fires). The heat was turned off, but when the teacher came over to check the disaster. Here was my pot black as tar at the bottom. She had a hairy fit and jumped up and down with rage on the spot. I apologised to her, but I don't think it registered with her and she then burst into tears. Eventually things calmed down and my fruit salad tasted great. It is something I still like to make even today.

We had our practical cooking exam at the end of the course, and I chose to make Scotch Eggs with salad, followed by apple pie and cream.

This I did with great nervousness, hoping that everything would turn out ok. Thankfully I passed the exam and gained a certificate.

Shortly after I had learned the tricks of preparing a meal, my father invited a couple who were friends of my Aunt Myra's. The wife had nursed with Myra years previously, and they had a son. He was a very clever lad who was well mannered, and this was a delight to me as most young boys in Glasgow around where I stayed were to be feared.

Anyway, I volunteered to make the meal for the visitors. It was salmon with lots of salad and potatoes with mayonnaise, followed by fruit salad and ice cream. If it sounds awful, it was. I prepared it with great precision arranging everything like a work of art on a large plate. When the visitors came, they were fascinated with the display of greens, tomatoes with serrated edges, peppers, and everything that went on Salad. The husband got his camera out and my cuisine was captured for eternity. We all sat to eat, me fluttering around the table like John Cleese in Faulty Towers. Just then, the young man got up from the table and was sick in the sink next to where we all sat. His mum rushed forward with her nursing skills to hold his head, and I was taken aback at this all happening over my masterpiece meal. When they left we all had a giggle at the poor guy and how my food disagreed with him.

CHAPTER 6

Hairmyres Hospital.

Once I left Logan and Johnstone Pre-Nursing College, I had to decide which hospital to apply to for nurse training. I had an aunt and uncle in East Kilbride, and thought it such a clean new town, so in my 17-year-old wisdom I applied to Hairmyres Hospital for acceptance. I was lucky to be invited to come for an interview, this entailed questioning about my thoughts on nursing, questions about my schooling, nursing college and then a medical examination for my weight, heart and lung health, urine testing, blood test and other exciting goings on.

I was told that I was too light weight to nurse. I was a 19-inch waist aged 19, so no doubt lighter than at 17. I ate enough to satisfy me and didn't think I had a problem. I decided at that moment that they were not going to burst my bubble, so I suggested they gave me a month's trial and if I was rubbish then they could boot me out.

I was given a date in 1969 when I would be 17 and a half to start, and don't ask me why this odd age. Maybe it was when the planets were in alignment or when there was a new manager in the hospital, or when some genius calculated the correct age of entering a very hard training programme. I was only 17 so had 6 months to relax before I started.

I had a friend who went to apply for pediatrics nursing, and she too was accepted in the Sick Children's Hospital Glasgow, but not until 17 and a half. We both decided that rather than laze about for 6 months we would go and work in a hotel in Oban for that time.

I announced this great plan to my parents, and my dad suggested I stayed with my Aunt Myra and Uncle Archie for the six months. Myra was what we in Glasgow call a "Nippy Sweety." I loved her dearly she was my dad's older sister and retired as a nursing sister in an Oban hospital, she married the hospital joiner my Uncle Archie, a lovely tolerant Man with a great sense of humour. So off I went to Oban on the train, with only a couple of pounds in my pocket, a small suitcase, and butterflies in my tummy.

I was welcomed with a lovely meal at the other end of mince and tatties (potatoes) with carrots through them. We never had carrots in mince in Clifford Street. This was tasty I thought, and just as my plate was finished (I was a very slow eater then) it was whisked away by my Aunt. In true Hyacinth Bucket fashion, she proceeded to wash the dishes. I offered to help, but she declined my offer, and probably thought my Glasgow bugs would be all over them.

A discussion was had after eating that I would give £8 a month for rent to them, and I agreed and next day went to look for hotel work. Myra came with me but waited outside as I strolled into the Caledonian Hotel and asked at the desk if there was any work available. I wore the marvelous fashion of the day: mini skirt, high heels, stockings, and a smart jacket.

I felt confident that they would desperately need this skinny teenager for some kind of employment in their hotel. Who could refuse?

My bubble burst when I was told, "Sorry no jobs at the moment." The receptionist was an elderly lady with severe black rimmed specs, and a smile like Jack Nicholson on a good day. She examined me from top to bottom then back up and down again, I was not to be beaten.

On I went to the next hotel, the Columba Hotel on the pier with huge red towers and red brickwork. My aunt suggested I wore something maybe a little longer for the event, but my wardrobe was limited with only one skirt, one jumper, and one pair of shoes. She kindly offered one of her summer dresses. She was size 16 and I was size 0 so this would not happen.

Off I trotted to the next hotel reception. I walked in, with aunt staying safely behind. Nobody was around, then after I rang the desk bell a man came running down the corridor to ask what I wanted.

"I'm looking for work sir." Again, I was examined top to bottom, but with a sneaky wee grin.

"Oh", said he.

"We are actually looking for housemaids." I thought to myself, what the heck is that? He explained I would be cleaning the guest rooms, serving teas in the morning, and anything else that the hotel needed to function smoothly. "

"Start tomorrow, 7 am" he said. I thanked him and went to inform my aunt of my new employment. I think she was more shocked than me when I got the job.

I stayed for a month at Aunt Myra's. I was loaned a bike by her niece Margaret MacDonald another good friend of mine. One night the two of us slept together in a double bed laughing and chatting about Oban and people we knew. A knock came at the door and a hand stretched over to our clothes lying over the chair. Here was Myra saying, "I'll just give your smalls a rinse girls." Margaret and I stared at each other in disbelief, "Blooming cheek," said Margaret.

Then there was the time when I was asked to work later. I said I would be back to Myra's at 7pm. I heard dance music coming from the house when I got back, and I rang the doorbell umpteen times with no answer. I walked up the road to Margaret's house and came back around 9pm. When I said where I had been nobody believed me. Uncle

Archie went up to Margaret's to see if I was telling the truth, he apologised after for not believing me.

Shortly after that I saw Myra searching for something in her house, as if she had lost some minor thing and couldn't find it. This search went on for a week, until one day she said, "I thought you had taken it Iona." At that I was horror struck, to be thought of as a thief and this was the last straw. I told her shortly after that it would be easier for me to stay in the hotel with the other girls, there would be four of us in a room. She wasn't pleased and I felt a bit rotten, but I had to do what I thought would make life easier for me.

The room was in the attic. There was a very pregnant lady, a spinster lady, a rough diamond lady from Glasgow, and me. We all got on well. The rough diamond turned out to be a thief, and she stole my tips before I got to my rooms. Mrs. D was the chief supervisor and she discovered that I never got any tips, so she kept watch on my rooms. One day she saw the rough diamond sneak into my rooms taking the tips, I never made a fuss but must have lost a lot of money which I couldn't afford to lose.

I was told when I started not to speak to the courier, and there were bus drivers that stayed in the hotel. This shocked me as I thought most of them looked respectable gents. Seemingly the pregnant lady in my room had a night of passion with one of the drivers and hence the pregnancy. Sadly, the story was in the local paper, and the guy was married and committed adultery with her. This was such a scandal back in those days, and I felt so sorry for her she was due her baby the next week or so when I was there.

One night she quizzed me after a long shift about who was gossiping about her. "Nobody" I said, which was true. She pestered me for ages asking who, who, who, who, and this went on for ages. My answer was always nobody. After some time I said, "Well if that's what you think then maybe it's true there is talk if it makes you happy, but no there is not." Stupid words from my mouth caused her to come down the next morning and start to thump one of the girls who she hated.

I was scared for her baby and escorted her upstairs. I felt responsible for the outrage, but there again I felt I hadn't said anything wicked. Everyone wanted to know who said what to her, and I kept quiet, but felt how stupid things are when words get twisted.

There was romance in the hotel with staff and guests, and I discovered that one of the porters had a crush on me. I was cleaning his room he shared with another porter. I got £7 for this job. I changed the sheets, dusted, cleaned the washbasin and other stuff when he walked in. I chatted to him and then allowed a kiss--a big mistake.

Before a minute passed there was a loud knock at the door, someone shouting my name and telling me I was in big trouble being in a room with a porter. My heart stopped, I ran out, and you couldn't see me for dust. I was just saved from the Casanova. He was extremely handsome, and fancied his Barra, as we say in Glasgow.

The next day I was cleaning the main stair, I turned and here was the bold boy sitting having tea with a girl. I stared at them and felt sad for her that he was really a cheater. This wised me up to how males can take advantage of daft girls like me.

My mum never told me about boys and how to keep them away from your body until married. I didn't really know about how babies were made. I knew the anatomy from school, but never realised the bits fitted together. After that I was on my guard. I had only kissed him but thought it could have been worse. I could have ended up pregnant, no husband, no nursing future, and Myra's reputation in shreds.

I decided I was going to watch my step with the opposite sex. Then I met a lovely lad in Oban, handsome, full of laughs, and stayed with his mum. He loved that song "The Boxer", and he introduced me to his mum, a lovely lady. We went on walks, and he took me to a disco. I left early because the flashing lights made me dizzy, and he wanted more than a kiss. I said it would be better if you knew I didn't want to have sex but wait until married. He was so upset but respected my wishes. I wrote to him from Glasgow, but we fell apart and I married someone else. Some things are not meant to be.

Hotel work was hard going for me cleaning rooms all day long, and dusting everything in sight. I was always exhausted after my shift-- 7am till 3pm, one half day off only. At the end of the season, we got a £30 Bonus which was such a treat and well appreciated. The owner of the hotel I discovered later was at school with Myra. He worked in the attic of the hotel and his brother was the cook. It was a nice place then and a happy interesting experience for me. I was sad to leave but glad to start my new nursing career.

CHAPTER 7

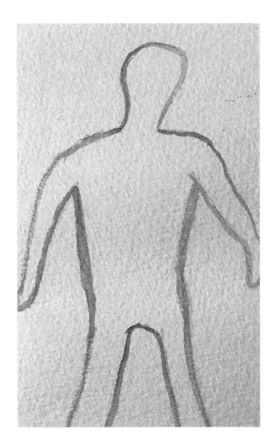

Hairmyres Hospital

I signed up for a three-year course to become a state registered nurse. It was a combination of practical experience and then nursing school. A uniform would be provided with a cape for warmth. A list of necessities was sent to me a few weeks before--sewing thread and needle, underwear, handkerchiefs, shoe polish and brush, toothbrush, toothpaste, sanitary wear, deodorant--the list went on.

I made a point of having every item. Dad bought me a black vanity case for all my stuff, and I packed the case with my day clothes. Dad took me to the nurse's home, and when we arrived the matron greeted us with a welcome and handshake and she said my room was upstairs. Dad went to lift the heavy suitcase up for me but was told men were not allowed in the nurse's quarters. I felt like a wee nun climbing up stair to be shown where I would stay for the next three years.

There were three other girls in the RGN Class and six EN Girls. The EN was a two-year course and I made friends with all the class. One great friend I made, Norma Holmes, now lives in Australia. I'm still on Facebook with her, and she is one of my favourite people.

We were all very nervous about our work ahead and none of us felt confident about looking after very ill patients. Our tutor Miss Wise was lovely and gave us all such good advice. There was also Mr. Stewart, he taught us most of the time and each day he would bring to class a drawing of a blank body. He would fill in each anatomy system we were to learn. He was very serious but informative about his teaching.

One day we dressed the skeleton at the back of the class with a nurse's uniform. It was the only time we saw him smile, apart from when he played the piano at a concert we all went to.

Word came round the nurse's home that there would be a talk from a scripture union member that night. I decided I wanted to go as I loved to hear the stories from the Bible. I walked into the room in full uniform and in walked the speaker. It was my old registration teacher from school (the one who gave me lines for chatting every day). He looked so shocked to see me, "You!," he said. I smiled sweetly and said, "Surprise."

You could have knocked him down with a feather, and it turned out his wife was one of my tutors. I'm sure they had a great chat about me later, and he thought I would never achieve anything in life. She knew my marks for nursing were excellent and I was a late bloomer I suppose.

We had a talk from a lady who worked for the Tampax company, a retired nurse. Someone told me don't laugh in her class as she would make you come out to the front and demonstrate how to insert a Tampax. It took all my stamina to sit with a straight face during her talking of female hygiene, washing your nightdress every day, and personal hygiene all with words of great gusto.

I could have died laughing but thankfully behaved.

The next day we were to have Mr. Stuart for instruction in the clinical room, where we learned how to give injections in oranges, make beds, turn unconscious patients and CPR. I walked toward the class door but stopped before entering. I could hear the mad Tampax lady's voice on a tape recorder. Mr Stuart was in convulsions of laughter listening to every crazy word. I knocked the door loudly and waited before opening it, giving him time to switch off. He did after all have a sense of humour and was not the serious soul we all thought.

My first ward was 21, brick walls with no paint on them, ten beds each side, and no privacy for any patients. Bedpans were timed so that everyone got one at the same time with just screens round the front of the main door, not individual screens. They were on wheels and there was not enough to go round each patient. It was mostly elderly ladies, and no mixed sex wards in those days thankfully.

The sister was always in her office so the staff nurse ruled the roost. She was very helpful to me, full of buzz and excitement, and she rushed around the ward like someone on roller skates. I was to take out my first stitches she informed me. I got on my white gown and mask ready to do the job ahead. It didn't worry me at all until the poor lady who was rather large exposed her mastectomy wound. It was a row of about 20 black silk stitches each one looking back at me like dead flies. I was to take out alternate stitches with aseptic technique that I had been taught in school.

Everything went fine, and I reassured the lady that the stitches were nearly out and all would be well for her. The wound had leaks here and there and it looked infected to me. I cleaned it and put on a new dressing.

"How do you feel," said the staff nurse who watched my every move. "I'm ok thanks" I said, after which I disappeared into the loo where I felt a bit dizzy. I pulled myself together and worked on, and during break I told my friends about my first stitch removal. They replied that you are not meant to take out stitches for at least a year, and I had been flung in at the deep end but survived.

The buzz I got while going on duty to a hospital ward is hard to describe. It's not like any other job where you walk into an office and have a chat before work with your colleagues, or a cup of coffee to wake up, or check messenger to see if anyone wants to speak to you.

You are on your toes from the minute you walk through the ward door, and the smell of Hibitane, clean floors, disinfectant, and the sounds of patients and staff talking gives you a wakeup call that you are there to do an important job. Forget the dance, party, or friend's house you were at last night. Get all that out your head and think what needs done as adrenaline rushes through your veins.

Blood, guts, and gore never fazed me after that. The mastectomy lady survived also to fight another battle. We had lectures in nursing school from consultants and one of them gave a talk on blood and its different properties. He had a difficult accent to understand and spoke of Rebecees. We all looked puzzled throughout the lecture taking our notes of what he was saying, and when we left the school we compared notes on some of his odd words Rebecees. It turned out to be R.B.C.s (red blood corpuscles). We had all so many laughs at other words he said.

Another lecture was from a psychiatrist, and he stood at a table as though he was holding in the toilet, twisting his legs from side to side, and we all sat in amazement at this performance. He spoke about Sigmund Freud and how he had come to the conclusion that everything in the whole world was to do with sex. Being 18 years old I found this very difficult to believe. Politics, religion, school, family life, mental illness, the army-- all were to do with Sex. I tended to think he was just a dirty old man trying to wind us up, and when the nursing tutor entered the room he changed the subject to something else.

Another lecture was on contraceptives and all the different types. There was another group of male nurses listening with us on the subject. Then the lecturer passed round the class various scary looking items to do with the subject: Durex, coil for uterus, and rubber cap for top of cervix. I had to hand one to the male sitting next to me and I was totally embarrassed and I'm sure he was too.

I was working away in a surgical ward. It was adjacent to the intensive care ward. It was a new way of looking after extremely unwell patients. A doctor came running down the corridor to me from ICU. He looked panicked, and he asked if I would come and look after a little girl aged 9 years. I quickly told sister where I was going and then ran after the doctor, and he told me just to watch the girl's breathing and let him know if it changed. He meanwhile was on the phone to try and get theatre and surgeons for her.

Her wee tummy was extended, and it was obvious she was bleeding. I was told that a truck had gone over her in East Kilbride Town Centre, and her parents were just outside in the waiting area. I had only been by her side for 5 minutes at the most when her breathing stopped. I shouted on the doctor, and he came over and started CPR.

It was useless, she was gone, and we tried for ages to bring her back. She was pronounced dead. I had only been nursing a short while and thus I thought was the worst thing in my life I had ever seen. I had to return to my ward, but as I walked past where her mum and dad were sitting I saw the doctor tell them the awful news. My heart went out to them, but I had to put on a brave face and get on with my work. It's something that has stuck in my head all these long years. To lose a child must be one of the most terrible things in the world.

We were also sent to Leverndale Hospital, the awful place my mum had been a patient in.

I was to meet the charge nurse in the dining room first Day, in full Uniform at 7 am. There I met Mr. MacDonald with a very quick handshake and a request for me to follow him to his ward as he walked quickly out of the room. It was a fair walk to the male ward of long-term patients. He produced a very large key and opened a massive Victorian door. The smell hit me in the face. It was indescribable-- a cross between a bed pan and cow field.

The wards inside were long term alright, but so were the hygiene standards. Forty men were incarcerated in Mr. MacDonald's ward and all looked so sad and drugged to the hilt. They wore badly fitted suits with trousers halfway up their legs, and stains of food that James the First would be proud of. Everyone needed a haircut. Mr. MacDonald looked squeaky clean in comparison, and there is no way a young nurse like me should have been in there with all these men as it was terrifying.

My first job in the ward was to administer the medication. In general hospital it is a very strict procedure where you read the kardex for the dose the doctor has prescribed, check the patients wrist band for correct name, and then sign that it has been given. Mr. Mac said, "Oh, we don't bother with all that stuff here. The Patients will tell you what they should get."

He stood over me as I dished out largactil, tofonil, anti-depressants, pain killers, and many other very dangerous drugs with the patients instructing me all along. After the drug dealing scene, I asked Mr. Mac for the bathing book. He laughed loudly and said these people would have a heart attack if they had a bath and that doesn't happen here. They just wash at the sink in case of drowning. I then enquired about changing their bed sheets, and again a great laugh from Mr. Mac. "No, we don't bother about that here." My thoughts were I had arrived in a Scottish gulag where the poor souls were left to rot with bed bugs galore, head lice, and other uninvited beasties.

I stood and scratched at all this lack of basic hygiene and felt helpless to say anything against it. When you are young and scared you keep quiet. If it was now I would have made such a fuss for these poor souls. Mr. Mac then told me how some of the patients had arrived. ome 40 years previously with different mental problems. I wasn't allowed to read case notes, and some of them would have been hair curling I'm sure. He teased a patient with scissors, and the man had tried to circumcise himself once. When Mr. MacDonald showed him the scissors he ran in the opposite direction. Another had taken a hatchet to his sister and mother, another had killed his sibling, and the horror stories went on.

Mr. Mac explained that the drugs when introduced a few years earlier had change completely the way patients were managed. Before the drugs he told me the patients walked all day in a circle round and round with the male nurses in the middle holding truncheons. Anyone stepping out of place would be beaten to put them back in line. I couldn't believe my ears.

The wages were more for mental nurses than general ones, probably because of the dangerous job they did. There was also a tendency for the nurses to turn out like the patients, in other words mentally ill.

I spent three long weeks in that long term ward, and every day was as boring as the next. One day Mr. Mac asked me in the duty room to practice his favourite hobby of ballroom dancing. I refused point blank. Here he was with his pristine suit and shiny shoes. I was in uniform and certainly not obliging him with a tango or cha-cha. He went on and on until I said I would have to ask my tutor about his request, and he shut up after that thank goodness.

In the ward adjacent was a charge nurse about to retired. He had white hair and always chatted cheerfully to me each day as I passed his ward. He had lost his wife recently and was very sad about her dying of cancer. My heart went out to him. One day he asked if I would like to see some photos of her. I told him that would be nice and then he asked me to come to his house for tea and biscuits. I went in my civvy clothes, he chatted away ten to the dozen, and asked if anyone knew where I was. I told him my charge nurse knew. I mentioned he had kindly asked me for tea (idiot me so trusting and ignorant) and I stayed only half an hour and thanked him for his kindness.

Years later I saw his photo in the newspaper. He was a sexual predator. My guardian angel looked after me on my visit to his home. Looking back I could have been raped, killed, tortured, the lot. It was a lucky escape. Why don't adults tell us of the horrors that can happen to us? They think they protect us from things happening by being silent. Most young women then were ignorant like me of what could be done to you. I see why the Victorians always had a chaperon for ladies going out. They were never alone, and maybe they were right.

The next three weeks was the female ward. It was a short stay ward and had women like my mum not coping with family life. One poor lady caught her husband in bed with her daughter. She tried several times to commit suicide, and there was a broken glass window where she cut her wrists. One day she began to scream and shout, and I was told to keep away while four staff dragged her by the hair, flung her on a bed, and gave her an injection that knocked her out. I thought this monstrous treatment, but being young you just accept everything in front of you.

Another woman had severe epilepsy she had bouts of it each day. She I was told took illegal drugs and was having sex with every male in the hospital. On this occasion she was in the bath, and I went to go in to help wash her, but again was told to stand back. The nurses were checking her private parts for drugs or cigarettes. I was told I hadn't seen anything happen. This was all very scary for me to understand, and I couldn't wait to return to general nursing. We were taught never to speak of our work outside the hospital, which I never did until now. This was the 1960s and 70s and most of these people are now dead. I am now 71, so I don't think there is a breach of confidence.

The most frightening thing I saw in Leverndale was ECT (Electro-convulsive Treatment) where the patient is wired to a machine that produces an electric charge to the brain and is meant to help their mental illness. It is a terrifying experience for the patient, and I think also terrifying to watch someone writhing with electricity charging through them. I am not an expert on this treatment but it seemed medieval to me. It does change how the person behaves they say, but what a way to do it. Doctors do everything to help cure their patients. That is their main aim and the job they are paid to do, but sometimes one has to question is the treatment worse than the disease itself?

I found Leverndale a harrowing, frightful experience, especially at my very young age. I had to learn all the aspects of illness in humans, I understand that, but to send such a young person to somewhere like that I don't think was thought through completely by those in charge. To do it now at my age would not be a problem, and from what I have experienced in life I would cope with everything without fear or sadness in my heart. I would accept that some individuals are locked up for their safety and that of the public's.

Margaret Thatcher when in government changed all of these hospitals. Only the very unwell patients are kept in locked wards. The majority today are housed with the public in homes throughout the country. They have carers who assist and train them to cope with shopping, cleaning, and other household chores. It saves a huge amount of money for the government to do it this way, and I am sure there are a lot of success cases among them. It certainly is better than locking people up for lengths of 40 years or more.

Nursing Care Training in the 1960-70s.

We were disciplined excessively, but there was good reason for that. We were trained to look after patients who relied entirely on our care and treatment. Care of the dying was instilled in our heads so that we knew every part of it. Dignity and gentleness were a priority.

Bedridden patients were another training importance. Bed sore prevention was a priority, with frequent turning of these patients, and adequate fluid intake with recorded fluid chart for each patient. Incontinent patients were treated with dignity at all times, with frequent toileting given to them. Incontinence pads, if needed, were changed often.

For elderly who could not feed themselves, help would be provided to assist them. We were always watching their food intake and recording it. A well-balanced diet was given, and the kitchens then provided excellent food: chicken, roast beef, vegetables, fresh orange, or milk with meals. On top of that you could pop into the ward kitchen and make cheese on toast or scrambled egg for a new arrival. I recall making brandy, eggs, and warm milk for cancer patients. They loved their evening drink, and it would only be a teaspoon of brandy but was tasty.

Young patients had games, jigsaws, and other stuff to entertain them. Parents were allowed to visit at any time with them. Clean linen was essential and changed frequently. All beds were made with the envelope fold to the sheets.

Senior nursing officers paid a visit to every ward on every shift, checking that all nursing care was given to the sick. They were terrifying individuals, but we made sure every patient was looked after.

There was a senior nursing officer known as "Pea Green" due to the dark green uniform she wore. She always, always, found a fault in her ward rounds. It was coming up to Christmas and the wards were quiet this week. A student nurse was in charge of a thoracic ward, and she decided that pea green would have absolutely no quibble about her ward.

First she got to know the illnesses each patient had. Then their names, date of birth, the consultant involved, and what operation they had. Their beds were immaculate, and the wheels of the beds turned in, the blinds at the same height, and everything was in order for her Majesty Pea Green to inspect.

In walked the nursing officer. The student rattled through the patient's names, diseases, and everything that she could think of. Pea Green stopped at the desk stood and looked round the ward and announced, "Nurse there is a fly in this ward. Kill it," and then walked out. It was harsh but the training meant we were always on our toes for any mistakes as we knew we would get roasted by seniors if we didn't keep standards high.

When I was a sister there was a patient with skin that reddened easily-- a sure sign they are susceptible to pressure sores. I would put a chart at their bedside and instruct the nurses to turn the patient every two hours, and sign that it had completed and communicate with other staff the situation. Creams were a protective barrier put on the skin, and a special inflatable mattress was used to allow no skin to have contact for long on the bed. We provided a foam looking doughnut for those with delicate skin on the sacral area, fleece heel shoes for feet. Everything was used to prevent the very awful sores that can happen if a patient was in bed for prolonged periods of time.

In those days nursing was more about helping doctors conduct procedures, basic nursing care, communicating with relatives, and teaching the student nurses all we knew. This was all common sense, and the best nurses were those who had children, were middle aged, and hard workers. You could tell them a mile off, and they were slightly OCD, very clean and well groomed, never had earrings, coloured hair, long hair on shoulders, nail polish, or too much makeup. They looked smart in their uniforms always, giving a professional look about them.

I made some great friends at Hairmyres hospital and especially my dear friend Marie Sin Yan Too, a girl from Mauritius, an Island off the coast of East Africa. It was a very beautiful place which I visited and met up with Marie after not seeing her for many years. She is now in that heavenly place, but we kept in touch all that long time by Christmas cards and phone calls. After our monthly pay of £15, both of us would go out to a Stakis Restaurant in East Kilbride and enjoy a meal, after which we would go to the Cinema and watch the latest film. This was such a great treat to both of us after long hard-working shifts in the hospital. Marie would come to my family home most weeks where she called my parents mum and dad, they loved her too, and we enjoyed the occasional dance nights in Glasgow.

I spent two years at Hairmyres and was soon to sit my final exam. I didn't do well in my exams recently as a lot was going on in my head about my family's sickness. One day my dad phoned me at the hospital very upset about mum, and said he couldn't cope alone with her, and she was very difficult to live with. He wanted me to meet him at Central Station. I got off duty and travelled to meet him. He was sitting in a taxi with mum, and she would not move from her seat. I spoke quietly to her and encouraged her to come back home with me, and they had just been to Aberdeen for a short holiday where they honeymooned years previously. The whole holiday had been a disaster, and mum had attempted suicide on the beach. It was all very awful for my dad, and he told me that he needed help at home with her. At that moment I decided to give up my training for a while and help him cope.

The next day I returned to the hospital and requested a meeting with the matron. I explained my home circumstances to which she was appalled that I should leave nursing to help them at home. She tore into me verbally and said I had to put my hospital patients first. I was weeping inside at all this, but never broke down in front of her. I left her office so upset. As I came out the assistant matron, who had heard the conversation next door, told me not to worry or be upset, but to do what is right in life and not heed the words of Matron. It gave me such a boost and I realised that the right thing was to leave and look after my parents. I did and was incredibly sad to leave friends and happy days behind me. I never felt for a moment I had made the wrong decision as mum was happy to have me home again and her state of mind improved a lot.

Dad

Stuart, Nicole, Ewan, Piper

Myra and me

Aunt Eileen

Me age 3

Scott, Heather, Stuart

Staff of Western Infirmary

CHAPTER 8

Ironing

Glen Har then back to nursing.

I needed a job near to my family home, so thought I could work at Hillingdon Estate just a bus ride away. I dressed smartly and in those days you could walk into a place and just ask for work, or write a letter of introduction to the personnel manager. It was simple and easy to get employment then.

I called at the first factory; a clothing manufacturer called Glen Har. I spoke to a Mr. MacDonald who was the big boss. I told him I had been nurse training and was looking for employment where I could spend time at home looking after my parents at night, where the hours were the same each day, and he told me they needed pressers. I didn't know what this involved so jumped at the chance of a wage and employment.

I started work at 7.30am which was very early for me. I had been used to shift work where you get a long lie in the morning if you were on backshift. One of the men that worked in the factory offered me a lift, and he said he picked up two other women at 7am across the road from me. I checked with the women if he was ok to travel with as I didn't like the thought of a middle-aged man driving me on my own. It turned out he charged me ten shillings for petrol and it worked out cheaper than the bus.

I got in his car the next morning. There were a lot of roundabouts on the journey and he went round them at top speed. My head leaned on the passenger window several times, and he drove ridiculously fast all the way there. My stomach was churning big time.

The work was steam pressing. An iron weighing 9 pounds was used to press the seams on coats before the lining was stitched on. I was only about six and a half stone in weight myself so found the work really hard and sore on my arm. The boss said not many girls stayed on at that job for long and I could see why. He was surprised I finished the shift and worked at a good speed. There were three other girls alongside me, but nobody spoke a word.

I got home and decided I would look for another job. While I was out searching for it mum told me that someone from Glen Har called to offer me a better job in the office doing button counting. I phoned to say I would come back and do the work, and that was my job for a Year. I also did some nursing work there taking needles out of fingers. It looked so painful with sewing needles right through the index finger of seamstresses. I pulled them out, gave them paracetamol, and advised them to get tetanus and penicillin at casualty. They never did and just went back to work straight away.

I worked in the medical room seeing to minor cuts and accidents. A girl came in one day and asked for painkillers as she was menstruating. I told her to lie on the couch for ten minutes until the paracetamol took effect. She did but just then in came the boss and screamed at her for skiving. I got told off for being too soft with the girls, so in future nobody bothered me much about medical problems.

I worked in a small office with a very nice gent who looked after orders for material, buttons, thread, and other materials to make clothes. He treated me really well and always was respectful to me. The work was really boring compared to my hospital training. It was soul destroying and although the people there were all very pleasant I could never feel any job satisfaction. The money was better at sixteen pound a week compared to my training, and that was a treat.

The big boss came to visit one day and had one or two girls try on coats to see how they looked. I was asked to model for a long coat that was the new fashion. I walked up and down the floor showing this coat and turning round in a model pose at the end. The big boss said I could have a job modelling. I refused his offer although he would have paid me loads more for the job. I decided I had to get back to nursing at that point. Mum and Dad were a lot better, so it was my time to restart training.

I went for an interview to restart nurse training in the Glasgow Western Infirmary. It was only a quick journey from my parents home if anything happened. They were happy to have another nurse who had some experience of the job so started me the following week.

I stayed in the nurse's home which the Hospital preferred in case of a major disaster or other. I would be there on hand, and they could also keep an eye on what I was up to be it studies or outdoor activities.

I quickly discovered that it was the opposite from Hairmyres. There were strict rules with men in the nurse's home. As I came off duty the first night, I passed two or three young men obviously visiting nurses. This made me feel a bit uncomfortable, as they were complete strangers to me and I didn't think it right that they should have been wandering around at their ease. I made sure my door was locked always before I went out. It was not that there was anything to steal but just the thought of them snooping around meant I never felt safe in the bath when I came off duty. I could understand why Hairmyres had strict rules on males visiting nurses.

The western uniform was old style and very practical. The dress was mid-calf length with long sleeves and starched white cuffs. There were 6 white buttons at the bottom of the sleeves, and these allowed you to roll them up when working. To answer the phone the sleeves had to be buttoned up and cuffs on. There was also a white starched apron with white belt, a stiff starched white collar, black stockings, black leather shoes and a crisp white starched cap while not forgetting 4 white hair grips to hold it on your head.

The nurses were inspected before going on duty, and you would be sent back to your room if anything was not right--even a brown hair grip caused a discipline. It made us realise that everything had to be correct with no sloppiness. There was no makeup, no painted nails, no earrings, and no necklaces. It was a way to show who was in control and a discipline that we respected.

Although the uniform sounds most uncomfortable, it wasn't. You could bend and stay respectable looking from the back, you could change your apron if soiled, as it often was. You always carried a spare apron.

It was warm in winter and cool in summer, but most of all it looked the part and gave an image of cleanliness and professionalism. They changed the uniforms not long after I qualified, and it became a white dress. This was ridiculously impractical. For one thing you could see through it, and you would stretch up for an IV. What you had for breakfast was seen from behind, as it was short, and you had to change the dress if it soiled.

I got measured for the new dresses when the arrived, I was a size skinny then. I wore it for a week, and the laundry lady had issued me with a size 18. I wondered why I was so uncomfortable, when her colleague saw me she told me to come in and get remeasured. She gave me their smallest size 10, and it was still baggy, but an improvement.

One of the first nights I was on duty in a ward the sister came up to speak to me. She said there were three nurses found with men in bed with them in their rooms and would not be on duty that night and the wards would be short staffed. Maybe Hairmyres had the right idea.

I did about a year's night duty my first year, probably because I had some training. One of the wards I went to I didn't get a report on the patients as the staff nurse was exhausted. Her words were, "Good luck." This did not fill me with enthusiasm as there had been twenty admissions that day and all very unwell patients in the male ward.

I started to do a bed round which was always done first to settle everyone down for the night's sleep. This was interrupted by a man in the first bed having a cardiac arrest. There was only myself and an auxiliary nurse there, and I got her to call the crash team (this was a group of doctors and nurses highly trained in life saving). Thankfully they brought all their equipment and had started cardiac massage with the patient, and he began to come round from no pulse or blood pressure to a nice pink healthy colour.

He was alive and they took him to the ICU and I continued on with drug administration and recordings. Shortly after another man took a cardiac arrest. Again, the crash team were called out, and they thought it was a mistake they said they had answered the call for that ward. Nurse said this is number two of the night, and after a good half hour it was obvious the man was not going to come around.

I phoned the office and asked for help to get my patients settled. A sister arrived and she started to move an oxygen cylinder the same height as herself. It rolled off the carrier and landed on the wooden floor bouncing about six times and sounded like thunder. The night just got worse, and the night sister went round to check the other patients.

She said, "Nurse, there's a patient in the top bed lying dead. I've pulled the screens round him." I could hardly believe that three men died on my watch all within a short time. I suppose a lot of nurses would leave training at that point, but my thoughts told me this was my calling and I had to continue even although it was very hard to deal with such traumas.

I also was trained that when you leave to go off duty you never take what has happened in your day home with you. Leave it at the ward door, and because of this I was able to do well and therefore cope with all the happenings in the hospital.

At that time in the late 60s early and 70s, Glasgow crime was at its highest. Stabbings were everywhere with all ages and races. Razor wounds, or as they call them "Glasgow smiles" were common. This was when a person is cut on both sides of their mouth to look like a smile.

My next adventure would be casualty. I enjoyed it very much working there, and a great queue of casualties would be sitting in a row outside the treatment area. It was only separated with screens, and the patients were seen quickly. I became an expert at bandaging within a few minutes cut fingers, cut heads, cut arms, and everywhere else you could imagine.

One day I was working with a stab wound patient and it turned out the boy who stabbed him was in the next curtained area. He jumped through the curtain and brought out his knife again, attempting a further stab wound. I was grabbed by a quick-thinking doctor who took me away from the scene and both boys were separated and put in different areas. Thankfully nobody was hurt and we all continued working away as though nothing had happened.

Each patient received anti tetanus and penicillin then, just in case of blood poisoning, Tetanus was an arm injection, and penicillin was on the buttocks. I recall a 6ft 6 inch man having this done. When I told him to lay on the couch for his posterior injection, he refused said there was no need. As I drew up the vial I heard a thud behind me, and he had fainted on the floor at the sight of the needle.

I always think there is no such thing as a "Hard Man." It's just a face they put on for those around them, like the Glasgow gang member that came in for a nasal manipulation (to fix a squint nose after a punch). He started to walk out the ward and said he didn't want the operation. I explained that he would be going around years later with a nose that looked odd if he didn't come back to get it seen to. He came back in and I escorted him to theatre.

I was moved to female medical ward day duty after that. The chief consultant was D.B. Brown, a huge doctor with hands like shovels and everyone was terrified of him. Patients were not allowed to read the newspaper during his ward round, and they had to sit straight in bed. He roared at a young Indian doctor for wearing sandals on duty and told him to buy leather shoes for his ward.

He would arrive in theatre and look down from the balcony at the operation in progress. One day he was watching myself and other doctors working away, and the senior doctor whispered, "Don't look now, but God is watching your every move." We all had a giggle. Another day he was performing a bowel operation and was holding the suction catheter. It came loose and the contents of the patient's bowel landed on his boot. Let's just say he was a very angry man most days.

It was part of my job to clean up after everyone had gone, and so this day I was scrubbing away thinking I was the only soul in the theatre. I started to sing to myself the beautiful Highland song "The Isle of Mull" I was in full thrust of high octaves when a deep scary voice shouted, "Nurse come here!"

I ran through to the area of the voice, and low and behold it was D.B. Brown himself, the fear of the hospital, and he who must be obeyed. I could have passed out at that point. He asked where I heard that song, and I told him my mum was from Oban and my Dad from Easdale Island. They sang it to me when I was young. He asked their names, and I told him. "On with your work nurse," was his next statement. I went to visit my parents and I asked my mum if she knew a Donald Brown. "Oh yes, he was from Kilmore just outside Oban. He went out with my Sister Joan," she told me.

The next day I was walking along the corridor and who walks toward me but D.B. He came up to me put his arm around me and told me he knew of my family and asked how they all were, then walked on. This was viewed by many staff on the ward, and I never let on why he spoke kindly to me. They all treated me like the Queen after that, as I said earlier there is no such thing as a hard man.

I loved the surgical wards although very busy every day, they were different. Some very ill patients after major surgery were put in the same wards as drunks who came in with head injuries. I always looked after all according to their illness. The drunk would be someone's son, Dad or other I used to think. They had to have quarter hourly recordings looking for signs of brain bleeds, and there were usually five or six of these men in a ward.

The cholecystectomy patients all needed a lot of post operative care. In those days if it was a huge operation with a large wound, complications had to be looked for often, with tubes for drains, intravenous drips, naso gastric tubes in their nose and all took time to observe.

One patient came in with a knitting needle up his penis, and he said it fell off the mantel piece. I was on night duty that time and the duty nurses would sit round the fire in the middle of the ward. Most sat and knitted, and we all whispered to each other. The only sounds were from the men snoring, passing flatulence, or dreaming. That night we all nearly jumped out our skins when the knitting needle man leapt out

71

of his bed next to us and began shouting for the toilet. The older nurses knew how to deal with him, but I was shaken about the fright we got.

Alcohol was a big problem in Glasgow in those days. We had a patient who came in after he was picked up by the police in Central Station. He was covered in faeces and drunk as a monkey. The sister told my colleague and I to take him to the shower room or delouse room as they called it. We got on white gowns with caps and masks and proceeded to shower him down in a wheelchair.

He sang away happily probably thinking we were a couple of prostitutes dressed as nurses, and we cleaned him up well after an hours work. Some weeks later I was getting lectures in the wards from the lecturer and about six of us were around a bed chatting about a patient's condition. We were all in civilian clothes, and I saw a man who looked awfully familiar walk by. He wore a posh blue silk dressing gown with cravat, hair brill creamed to perfection, and red velvet slippers. I realised it was the drunk we had cleaned up weeks before. What an amazing transformation I thought.

Nursing was not all seeing sadness and gloom around you. It was extremely satisfying when a patient make a good recovery and they were allowed home. In those days people were kept in for a long time, periods of ten weeks in some cases depending on the recovery. It was not like today where most operations, even major ones, patients are home within a week or day cases for less serious procedures.

The teamwork with nursing and medical staff was tremendous, and we all supported each other. In saying that, student nurses were never allowed to speak directly to doctors then. If something was to be brought to their attention you had to tell the staff nurse, and first names were never used either. At meals all grades sat at tables with their own fellow grades, sisters at one table, staff nurses another. and students never with doctors or senior staff. It meant we all knew our place and were never familiar with staff of lower grades.

I did feel it harsh for auxiliary nurses. They were never given training then, but most were married women who had experienced life more than any of us. They had children and families with elderly parents to care for, and they were really the backbone of the hospital. All of them were hard workers with lots of common sense, and they were so good at giving young nurses like myself advice and guiding us through our working day. Yet some of the seniors treated them as low life as a lot were tough Glaswegians from rough areas.

I did always feel though they were the real nurses, and they saw to most of the dirty jobs: bed pans, bed baths, cleaning bed linen, and other not so good jobs. Even when I became a ward sister I never opted out of doing these jobs. To me that was real nursing, cleaning the outputs of the human body is not pleasant but essential work. Faeces, urine, bile, sputum, blood, pus, and other unmentionables were always smelly and unpleasant, but dealt with professional care for the patient and respect for their privacy.

Large drainage bottles filled with yuck had to be emptied, urine bags, drainage bags and others also. That's why maybe today in my old age I adore perfume and the sweet smell of roses and flowers. We all wore perfume on the ward and it was never strong but sprayed below waist. The first thing we asked each other if on a backshift after the report where we all stood round the desk was what perfume are you wearing.

The patients were kept clean each day, and a bathing book was in every ward. This showed who got baths, bed baths or showers, and they were weighed on admission and when discharged. Their hair was checked for nits or lice, skin was checked for scabies, spots, rashes, and previous or current scars.

One day on the children's ward I was asked to do the heads. This involved me dressing in gown and rubber gloves with sleeves tucked in. I was in the middle of examining a new wee girl whose parents were very important people. In fact, one nurse said to me she didn't think I needed to look at her, but I was told she had to be examined like the others by a senior nurse. When I looked at her hair which was grown down her back, it was alive with nits and lice crawling everywhere. I quickly told the sister and she had to be discharged right away and given another date for admission.

I worked with an Aberdonian nurse once, and she was hilarious. One day she came running into the sluice with a fist closed, opened it under my nose and said, "Look nursie, a huge louse from that man in bed 15." Here was a beastie (Glasgow word for anything that crawls) and it was crawling in circles in the palm of her hand. You would think she had just killed a stag at Balmoral Estate the fuss she made. The poor patient had to be bathed disinfected and rubbed down with lotion to clear his problem.

We always had a bath, and never a shower when we came off duty. A bath killed all bugs if they managed to arrive on you. Fleas were a huge problem as they could jump from one person to another. The telltale red spots were a sign. Now that you are all scratching furiously, I'll change the subject quickly.

We were never encouraged to see patients outside of work, and we kept our work separated from our home life always. I did know a nurse who married her patient who was paralysed from the waist down and she had been at nursing college with me.

There were parties in the hospital at night or at someone's home. I was invited to some, but never liked to mix work and pleasure as it always fails and can ruin your reputation completely. I did go to parties with friends from my childhood though, but they were mostly University ones (all my pals were clever).

I met my future husband at one of these, and his first question to me was, "What newspaper do you read?" This I think was to discover my intelligence level. I told him all of them, and he looked shocked. I explained I was a nurse and when I went for tea break I would ask a patient for a loan of their newspaper. It could be a Daily Record, The Sun, a Glasgow Herald, The Times, The Guardian-- you name it. This impressed him I think, so he arranged to meet me for a date.

Chapter 9

The Western Infirmary.

Joe was very handsome, funny, and made me feel good. He was a bit of a "Toffee Nose" I thought but was a reader of books. He was at University of Glasgow and had lovely parents who were down to earth people whom I grew to love dearly.

The first date I said I would meet him at Boots corner. I had forgotten that I had also been invited to a friend's birthday party the same night. I told her I really like this boy but didn't want to let her down. So on the first date I took my friend Marie (Chinese Mauritian) and Indeera (Indian) to meet him. It was like the League of Nations Meeting with umpteen races present. He wasn't fazed and the plan was he would take me to the cinema, and we would go to the birthday party after.

The party was in Minerva Street, just along from where he stayed and from the hospital. All went well and we both had a good night. The party was no alcohol, and there were all races of people there. I didn't know in those days how respectfully dressed women should be around Muslim men.

I wore a silk trouser suit which covered me from top to bottom. I was complimented on my dress sense often that night, and we danced to the Beatles and all the pop music of the early seventies. Food was plentiful, various sausages, sandwiches, and sausage rolls. It was a banquet to me, and I had never seen so much food in my life. Everyone enjoyed chatting to each other, skin colours were never a problem we all had respect for everyone and nobody felt awkward or alone.

Romance with the boyfriend was just a kiss goodnight, and my friends were my chaperons and I got back to the nurse's home around 11 pm with thankfully a day off the next day.

Life was happy, with hard work, but with meeting lots of people working in different wards every six weeks I soon lost my shyness and enjoyed all the new adventures of youth.

I visited home when I could, and I brought the boyfriend back to meet my parents. He invited me for a meal to meet his parents, and my friend Marie came also. His mum was a great cook and made roast beef for us. This was a great treat for both of us and we all got on well. They looked on me as a daughter which was lovely.

Joe and I were in love and engagement was soon to happen. Not long after we met he failed his final exams at University and became unemployed. I tried to support him through this difficult time, and his parents were so upset about it. The real reason he failed was he got in with some clowns at University that didn't need to study to pass exams and they drank alcohol and partied most nights. Study was never done so when the exams came round they all passed but he didn't.

I was still working long hours at the hospital and tried to juggle boyfriend, parents, and work together. It became a lot, and my dad complained that he never saw me. I visited when I could manage. He didn't realise the shift work, night duty, seeing my friends, or everything happening around me kept me so busy. It was soon to be my 21st birthday, but it was just another day to me.

I was on a busy gyn ward at the time doing night duty. I had not asked for time off as I knew how busy and short staffed they were. When Joe the boyfriend discovered I'd be working on my 21st he was appalled. My dad also was upset that I would not see my family on my birthday. I said I would celebrate on my days off.

I worked through the night, and it was very busy and I was exhausted going off duty. Joe phoned to say his parents had some cake and champagne for me. I had to wash and go up to their house which was a good mile walk up a hill. I got there and they had gifts, balloons, bottles of drinks and cake. I felt embarrassed and stayed only an hour.

When my dad found out he was annoyed so much that I had not spent time with them. I never meant to cause upset, and I felt I had been forced to see Joe's parent on my birthday. When you are young you get talked into doing stupid things and making daft decisions, but it's meant to be I think. My parents and Anna got me a beautiful pearl ring for my birthday. I treasure it even today.

I never suffered back pain in my youth, but many nurses did. Part of our job then was to make sure patients never got sore lying in bed. They were lifted and turned often, doing this to some twenty patients twice a day was an epic job. Some of the ladies were very heavy, and one I recall instantly in my mind was 28 stone lady. We had to phone the porters to put her on a bedpan, and six men came up from the porter's office and helped me to position her for toileting. This must have been most embarrassing for her, but the nursing staff were busy elsewhere and would not have the strength. She never bothered though and being Glaswegian made a great joke of it.

My feet were always aching through walking up and down the long Victorian wards. Varicose veins are my signature for nursing today, along with bunions, and duck shaped feet. This is something that still shocks assistants when I go shoe shopping.

A night I recall with great clarity was the murder that happened on my shift. It was around 9 pm and I was working in acute surgical receiving, meaning anyone who needed emergency surgery was brought to my ward. I had 6 beds ready with admission pack made, and I received a phone call from the night sister that a patient was arriving very soon with massive stab wounds and I was to prepare for his admission.

I quickly got a drip stand, wound packs, plastic bags for his clothes and waited. Then I heard a great commotion in the corridor as he was being wheeled straight to theatre. His condition was critical and time was of the essence, and he would not come to my ward at that time. I looked out along the corridor and all I saw was a bed with not a bit of mattress showing with a massive pool of blood covering it all. I was so shocked and horrified and it made me shaken to see it and to think this was done by another human being made it worse.

The surgeons worked on him through the night trying as they would to stem the blood flow, but to no avail. After 9 hours in theatre he was pronounce dead. The theatre staff brought his clothes in a plastic bag to the ward, and they were red in colour. I put them In a cupboard with his name on them for safety. Later a policeman arrived and requested them for evidence in a murder trial. A few weeks later I had to go to Maryhill Police Station and identify them. It was all so gruesome, and he had been a young man in his thirties. His life was suddenly taken away, probably in a silly fight and drink involved. Life was cheap in Glasgow then.

Death can be a frightening thing to see when you are young and have never seen it before. A case comes to mind when an elderly patient stopped breathing. I called the doctor as the man had just been recovering from a laryngectomy (removal of the larynx). His colour was blue due to lack of oxygen. The doctor quickly put the ambubag over his mouth to give him air. I recalled that the airway to the mouth was stitched up in that operation, and told the doctor to put it over the patients tracheotomy hole, which he did. The man went a lovely shade of pink and breathed away fine. It was such a great moment and felt so wonderful to bring someone back to life.

Night duty was a constant feeling of extreme tiredness I recall. Sleep was little as there was always noises around in the nurse's home. I hardly ate food as even my appetite was suppressed most days.

One ward I was sent to was the Gardiner Institute. This was combined with research in the University next door, and it was for investigating diseases like Cancer, Leukemia, and other nasty illnesses. The ward sister was to be feared by all including the senior staff, and she was only about four and a half feet tall, had a tongue that would open a wine bottle, and a temper like an elephant in musk.

This was the place I was to spend the following eight weeks. She loved men, was menopausal, and hated pretty nurses. She took unused bags of blood home for her roses, and to me this sounded like Mrs. Dracula herself. She was a spinster all her life and still on the hunt, and fear was all over me. A patient had died on her ward and when his wife came to the ward her words were to her were, "That's the way the cookie crumbles." Would you really say such a thing to someone in that situation?

Anyway, I went on duty early to her ward, just with an auxiliary and myself to look after 20 patients. We had about ten tests to do on patients at 5 am, collecting all their urine in large containers. We were testing those on fat reduced diets for ketones in their urine (a sign they are burning fat in their body). This was all very technical and complicated for me at that time. Anyway the shift went slow, with not much happening except me clock watching. I did all the tests, took recordings, wrote the kardex up, saw to the urine bottles, and made the patients comfortable.

We went in to check on something, and it was 7.30 am and Mrs. Dracula was due in any time now. Just at that a wee lady asked me for the toilet, and I walked her across the corridor and heard a splashing sound. She had diarrhea all over the floor. Just at that, guess who walked in? Yes, it was one of those moments in life when you wished you carried a gun to shoot yourself. I just said, "Oops, sorry about this sister, slight accident." She looked at me and I'll swear I saw her horns appear and she rushed off into her office and began to do her morning striptease from civilian clothes into uniform. She did this just in case a doctor walked in by accident, which happened often.

I was quickly sent off duty and ran all the way to my room where I put the dressing table in front of my door. She had a habit of waking nurses that hadn't put the right dot on a chart, and they would have to get into uniform and go down to her ward where they corrected their mistake. This was NOT happening to me, it never did.

Another night I was on and smelt burning. I phoned the fire brigade right away, then told the staff to get the patients ready to evacuate. Then I phoned the senior nursing sister on duty to tell her.

The fire brigade arrived within minutes, and I got a fright when I saw two of them dressed in their fire gear looking around the ward. It turned out there was a machine in the lab downstairs that went on fire. The fire men praised my quick action, and the night sister told me off for phoning them first. Life as a student nurse was always learning to ignore those who told you off I thought.

I also worked day duty on her ward for eight weeks. I don't know what was worse, as she had me clean cupboards, the sluice, and all the glorious dirty jobs of nursing. When a doctor came into the ward she would shush me away to clean a cupboard so that she could be the star attraction. All the time the doctor was trying hard to avoid her.

The ward had some very ill patients in it, and ladies with their jaws wired so as not to be able to eat solids. This I thought was so cruel and medieval, and most of them were extremely overweight. They would get home at the weekend, but that stopped when one lady liquidised a fish supper and sucked it through a straw. They were fed salad and vegetables only, weighed every day, but did lose weight. Dr, Now would have been proud of them (Dr. Nowsaradan, an American doctor that does surgery for the overweight people in America).

The saddest thing I saw was a wee girl of nine with Leukemia, she was slowly dying and had to be barrier nursed. This involved everything that went into her room being sterilized, which was not an easy task. We had to wear gowns and masks and one day her mum brought her a large teddy. The sister shouted at me when I went to bring it into the room.

"Nurse sterilise please." I had forgotten, and I certainly can thank sister for teaching me barrier nursing--something that is used with today's COVID infections.

The strangest thing happened just a couple of years later. Sister Dracula ended up as a patient in my ward when I worked in ENT. Somebody said to me, "Now's the time to get your own back on her," It's not how I roll and she was admitted with otitis media (a very painful ear infection). I let the other nurses attend to her and moved myself to the male ward mostly. Karma does happen so it pays to be nice to people.

I was then sent to gyn ward on the top floor. Glasgow gyn was different from when I had worked there in Hairmyres. Women with venereal diseases, broken bottles in vaginas, bruises from rape cases, miscarriages, and all the awful stuff that can happen to women.

On my first day there I was asked by an older nurse to get a bedpan for the lady in bed 8, I was just about to go behind the screens with the pan when another nurse stopped me,

"Which nurse told you to do that without gloves on." I told her who, and she then told me that this particular patient had gonorrhea, a very highly infectious type of venereal disease that spreads like wildfire, with contact. I was saved by a minute.

I also came across a young patient who had 9 children. She was in a room to herself and had serious cancer of the vulva. She had freesia talc in her room, and it had a strong smell of it everywhere. To this day I dislike the smell of freesias as they remind me so much of her.

Everything happening around me was sometimes very scary especially when I was so young and inexperienced. I always recalled the Red Cross motto to stay "Cool, Calm and Collected." This kept me sane in times of ghastly stuff going on. I was also taught in my training to walk a certain way in the wards, keep your hands folded together, walk with your head up high, back straight, and keep an invisible cocoon around you always. Look straight into people's eyes when speaking to them, and never get flustered. All these tips helped me deal with every event each day.

It's strange how some patients stick in your mind for all your life, and one of those was a lovely young man with skin cancer. He was in the surgical ward, his colour was dark grey, and he was very ill. For a few days fluid was aspirated from his lungs with a huge needle--a painful experience. His wife worked in the hospital and they had a 6 month baby girl. I remember seeing him sitting smiling and laughing with her on his bed, and she wore a pink nylon dress, and he worshiped her.

I was moved to another ward, so never heard how he was keeping. In those days nurses spoke about their patients, but never by name. I learnt his wife went home after a visit to the hospital to find that her house had been ransacked and valuables taken from their home. I recall thinking how can people do these sort of things? The staff in Glasgow put around a box for her to give her some money. That was Glaswegians at their best.

CHAPTER 10

Gandavon Sands

My next placement was in the Western Infirmary. I had still not much experience dealing with diabetic patients, or with medical wards, but here I found myself in charge of a ward for the first time. It was around 8 am and the consultant came round to check his patients, and he noticed that a Lady was behaving strangely. She was beginning a diabetic coma, where she needed either insulin or sugar.

I had just walked on the ward and was pretty clueless about these things. The senior nurse who was usually there was off sick, and the consultant was very kind to me, saying it wasn't my fault this happened.

He went down to the main senior staff office and gave them a telling off. Thankfully a senior nurse came to help me and all the diabetics got their morning insulin. Just then a sister came up to speak to me, and she said that I should never ever ask for help or for someone to assist me with work. I could not believe what I was hearing. I explained that I did not have much experience with diabetics, her attitude was that nurses should always be able to cope with any event. Looking back, she probably just had a roasting from the consultant and took it out on me.

Medical wards were busy places. An American patient who was recovering after a stroke told me that he had never had such excellent care when sick as in the NHS. He had been in many private hospitals throughout America, and not one came up to our standards in Britain.

I never think money and medicine are a good mix. My son today in Chicago area is still paying for the birth of his two children--one 7 and one 2 years old ($5,000 for each birth).

Today in Britain we still have the NHS, but in some areas it's on its knees with long waiting lists, poor staffing, and lack of discipline with nurses. Although there are still the stalwarts, the staff who are dedicated workers that give 100% to their job don't expect a lot in return.

When I trained, I got free board in the nurse's home. I got free food, I got my laundry washed free, if I took sick a consultant saw me that day. Nurses today are never treated like that, and they pay for all these things themselves with most having families now and outside commitments. They are always stressed, working shifts that are moving from night shift to day duty without sufficient rest in between. They still risk their lives each day and are still low paid but to keep the health of the nation afloat that is what they do every day. We must admire them totally.

The only social life I had at that time was with Joe my Boyfriend. He took me out to the cinema, to a meal, and to his parent's house for dinner. It was such a treat for me to eat at their house and his mum made a lovely meal always: roast beef, chicken pie, and chips that tasted super. I ate very slowly then and was still stick thin. I would take an hour to eat my food and could never finish the huge plate she gave me. Everyone would be finished eating and I was still plodding on, chewing every bit for ages, they all sat in amazement at this performance of mine, but I enjoyed it so much.

In the Western I never had a group of friends like Hairmyres. Most of my colleagues were busy with their own lives and friends, and even in the nursing school there was not the same friendship between them.

They seemed older than me and more serious in their attitude, but on the wards I got on with all of them.

My next placement was ear, nose and throat, or ENT as it was known as then. It was a happy place to work and all the staff were great. The consultants all spoke to you and a lot of the patients were children admitted for tonsillectomy.

The female ward was painted pink and always had vases of flowers on every bed table. There was the scent of roses, carnations, and other flowers. Vase cleaning was the student's job and I loved doing it. The water was changed every day and the vases were rinsed with soapy water to freshen them. A label was on most of the vases, but there would be an uproar from a patient if they got the wrong flowers.

Today in the hospitals flowers are not allowed any more, which is sad. A lot of the busy wards did not have time to clean the vases resulting in a lot of stinking flowers everywhere that would cause infection.

Theatre days were busy in ENT. Sometimes as many as 10 children for operations, and they kept the adults till the end of the theatre list as their surgery could last a few hours. When I qualified as an RGN (Registered General Nurse), I chose to work in these wards.

One day a patient came in for surgery as she had esophageal cancer. She arrived with her husband the day before, her operation took 9 hours, and when she returned from theatre I hardly recognised her. A huge piece of tissue covered her chest area, and she had a tracheotomy and looked so sick. I stayed on late that night to make sure she was comfortable and pain free.

The doctor came in and asked who was on in the morning. It was me. Sister had arranged her holiday to avoid the stress of looking after her. The doctor was not pleased, but said he knew she would be all right and in good hands as he trusted my nursing care.

One day a consultant came up to me and suggested I gave his private patient a little more care and attention compared to my other patients. I told him my patients were treated according to their needs and illness, not their bankbook. He thought this amusing and left quickly, probably wishing he had never mentioned that. He had a Rolls Royce parked outside and was doing more private patients than other doctors.

My thoughts are that doctors should have a contract to sign so that when they qualify they work only for the NHS that trained them for 7 years. They could pay to opt out if they wish, but to have a mix of private and NHS is wrong I think.

For years the health service was supported by dedicated doctors and nurses and they worked only for its survival. If they want to work private then they need their own equipment and supplies, and not using health service property. It also means that a patient paying private gets to go to the front of the waiting list. As I said earlier, money and medicine don't mix.

On the male ward there were no flowers, but men are good patients. Women like everything done for them when they are in hospital, especially if they have children, and are enjoying the rest, (not all of them, but in general).

A lot of the men had cancer. The word was never mentioned in those days. Patients were told they had a cyst or nodule, never the C word. It seemed a kinder thing to do, but the rules changed when a patient who was married sued a doctor for not telling him how ill he was. It meant he could make no plans and his wife and family would be left adrift with his death. So today doctors tell cancer patients every detail of what is about to happen to them, which I am sure fills them with fear and horror. Even operations today are spelled out in great gory details and to the poor soul listening it must sound like something from a horror movie.

I was about to go for my break one afternoon when I turned around to check all was well in the ward. I saw a patient who had recently had a laryngectomy pointing to his tracheotomy hole and looking a nasty shade of blue. I quickly called the doctor and sister. There was a suction machine at his bedside with instruments. The sister appeared and she started to panic. She asked him to sit down and relax which is not something you cannot do when you are gasping for air. I had a look at the hole on his neck and could see a piece of tissue. The suction outlet on the tube was at the side and usually is just for sucking mucus. I cut the end of the tube to make a straight hole and the sister looked at me in horror. I put it in to the neck and sucked out a 2-inch piece of tissue that was blocking the airway.

The patient took a huge gasp of breath and thankfully turned a lovely shade of pink. I put the oxygen mask over his airway, and he looked so grateful to me. He patted my back and thanked me kindly. In came the doctor and I showed him the piece of tissue. He could not believe what had just happened and the sister disappeared in disgust. After some years she was given promotion to senior nursing officer and would float around the hospital like the bees knees. It gave us all a giggle to see her, and I was fond of her as a person and enjoyed working with her. I always kept my Red Cross motto in my head. Stay cool, calm, and collected always.

I once was in theatre and a new doctor was learning how to give an anesthetic. There was a very smart female anesthetist showing her the ropes. The young student was shaking like a leaf as she inserted the endotracheal tube. The senior gripped her hand and told her, "You have been shown, trained, and know how to do this. You can do it no bother, with no thoughts that you can't, so go for it."

Her words stuck in my head and after hearing that I did think if you are trained, confident, and know what to do then just go for it. In saying this, I worked with a male nurse who ran into a cupboard when things went wrong. He was a joy to work with, but in an emergency he just could not handle it at all.

Additionally, I read a book about spread sheets, and how airline pilots get out of tricky situations. They have a spreadsheet with numbers, number one check cargo door shut etc. This plan is always followed to the minute and sees them through the situation, saving Lives on the way.

"Be Prepared" was another motto I learnt in Girl Guides. They said be always one jump ahead, make a plan, make a note of what you need to carry it out, don't rely on remembering things, as we always forget when a situation occurs. Then get things ready for every future event in your life, save for a rainy day, let your loved ones know what you want in the future, lay out your clothes the night before for important events the following day, and plan ahead always (especially if you work in hospital). In the hospital setting, this meant check you have enough staff coverage for major operations, check your stores have the right equipment, check relatives know what is going on with their loved ones, check everyone in the ward knows what is happening, and just think wide of the box. Make sure medicines are available for every event and the pharmacy knows about changes.

Sometime later I was in my last year in the Western Infirmary and about to sit my finals, and I was sent to the busiest top ward in the hospital--Professor Kay's Unit of General Surgery, where the crème de la crème worked. They only had senior staff in this ward, and I was sent there as I was to sit my final exams.

The operations were huge surgical procedures that required a lot of post operative nursing care. My work was cleaning wounds and doing dressings. Everything was done with aseptic technique with maybe 20 dressings each morning. I would be in gown and mask for most of the morning. There were a lot of leg amputations done, bifurcation grafts, hernia repairs, bowel surgery, arterial surgery, and many more.

I sat my practical exam for my finals in this ward, and I had lots of practice on dressings so found it very straight forward. The patient I got was terrific, Mr. Holiday. What better name to cheer me up? He knew it was my exam and so chatted away to me. I was to take out 20 stitches so managed without any hiccups. I had passed my practical and was so relieved.

Next came the written exam, and this was not my forte when I was young with so many diseases and treatments to learn. The nursing care for each one different. The thought of it all made me sick with worry. I hated exams at school, but this was worse. I went to Gartnavel Hospital to sit in a room for 2 or 3 hours, writing furiously about all the stuff in my head. To my relief it was all about nursing care, and what to do if a patient came in with no name, unconscious, and nobody with him. I wrote screeds of stuff, remembering the letters TLC (Tender Loving Care) that popped into my head. I passed with joy and could not have felt such a great relief ever in my life. I had failed the prelims due to the death of my dear Dad at the time, so to pass was such a joy.

Dad had died aged 52 of a cardiac arrest in the Southern General Hospital. I was shocked to get the news of what happened. Seemingly he was joking with the staff on arrival at hospital, but everything happened in a flash and they could not resuscitate him. He was called to heaven.

The funeral was in Easdale Church and all my aunts, uncles, cousins, and other family were there. Mum, Anna, and I stood at the front with his coffin draped in Rangers colours. My cousin asked if he could put them on his coffin, which he did. Dad had such a short hard life but left a lot of happy memories for us all to remember. He was my hero. I never really cried as I felt I had to be strong for Mum and Anna, also the nurse in me had to be a stalwart. Life continued without his happy face around and God gained a lovely person.

Mum and Anna moved to the west end, and they sold the Clifford Street house, my family home. The new M8 Motorway was being built, and houses were knocked down everywhere for it to stretch around the city. Our house was turned into a gable end, with nothing but air on the other side of it. Anna was staying on her own at this time, and I was working in the Western still.

Mum was in hospital again, and while she was there the builder put a huge hole in the wall of a cupboard while knocking down the adjacent houses. The ceiling all came down in the kitchen. Thankfully, Anna was not hurt, but I felt awful to leave her to deal with all that was happening. The ward was so busy to take time off was not an option. A shortage of staff with really unwell patients meant I had to be there for them.

Insurance were very good in those days and she had a claim each week for damage. I went to the Glasgow City Council to see if the work around our house could be averted. The man I spoke to showed me the plans and said nothing could be done. Looking back we should have got some kind of compensation for the disruption to life, but no, people don't ever use money in that direction.

Eventually Anna moved with mum to Apsley Street in the West End of Glasgow in a lovely flat one floor up. She decorated it so beautifully. I was happy they were out of Clifford Street, but sad to leave our family home behind.

The secret to happiness they say is to be able to adjust to change, be it moving house, death of loved one, divorce, ill health or other. We must learn to move forward, live in the NOW never the past, but that can be hard for some people to do. Life moved on.

CHAPTER 11

Marriage and Love.

I had been seeing Joe Mueller for a couple of years now but did not want to marry until my exams were over, so at this time he proposed we marry. I accepted with happiness as I loved him dearly and he gave me support in my life as a nurse. We got married in the August 19th of 1973. My dad was still alive at this time and he walked me down the aisle of Bellahouston Parish Church, the very church I had been attending all my life.

It was a small wedding as funds were short, but Jim insisted on a fine wedding as he was an only child. I did feel it was ridiculous to spend money on something we could not afford but bowed to his wishes. I could ask only my immediate family, aunts, and uncles. None of my cousins were there, or my friends from childhood, but you cut your cloth to suit your needs.

I was trying to organise the reception at this time. The dress was made by a friend of my mother-in-laws and cost only £5, the reception was £70, and it was a lovely day and everyone had a good time including Joe and I.

For some reason or other that night, I felt Joe had thought he made a mistake. As he sat across from me in a chair and had a look of fear in his eyes, he was quite aloof and I worried about his feelings, but never asked him why he looked so pensive in his thoughts.

We bought a one-bedroom flat in Elie Street just across the road from the Western, and my life was now very busy, Joe was not a helper around the house, so cleaning was my job on my days off. I also had the washing to see to, but thankfully there was a launderette just around the corner from us. For a couple of pounds I got our weekly wash done

90

quickly, but the effort of carrying it upstairs was a lot for me. It was extremely heavy and we were two flights up in the red tenement stone building.

I carried on full-time work and was still in Sir Andrew Kay's Unit as a staff nurse then. I enjoyed the work but felt even more exhausted coping with married life, housework, and nursing. I asked for a transfer to ENT. The sister took me into her office and begged me to stay, but sometimes in life you know where your spirit is going, and you follow your instincts.

A week or so later I was welcomed to Dr. Mackinlay's ward on the top floor. He was a lovely man and worked well with me every day and was always appreciating what I was achieving. There were several other consultants in the unit with all excellent and professional doctors. Even the junior doctors were great, and we were a super team. We gave our all for the patients, staying late after our shift ended, working split shifts when short staffed, everyone got on well a made the unit such a happy place to work in.

I rotated from male to female wards depending on the staff situation, there was a quick turn over of patients each week. One day while on duty I admitted a young man. His face was purple with severe bruising and broken nose. He was taken to theatre for nasal correction or as it is called--this is basically straightening a squint nose. It was New Year and there were more visitors in the ward than usual at visiting time. Usually rules were strict in those days about visitors. It was two people only to a bedside then, but this day, New Years Day, was a happy time for Glaswegians who celebrated New Year big time. The patient was being observed for head injury or other bleeding to his head, so I went to take his recordings, and at that he began to rouse.

He had not been awake since admission so was confused at where he was. He then tried to get out of bed, saying he would go home, but he was in no fit state to do that. I put my arms around the bedpost and his waist as the other nurse on duty with me was on a break. I could not hold him like this for long as he was a big guy, and my arms were aching.

I had not alternative to shout for help, before I knew it six visitors (men) all came to my rescue, grabbed a hold of the patient, and flung him on the bed. At this time I was asking them to be gentle, but they were as gentle as a pack of Lions. The visitors had been desperate to help me as I struggled for a good three minutes with the poor guy. They were there when I shouted, and all became calm. The doctor was called, and more sedation was given to my patient. Eventually he ended up in Woodilee. I escorted him to the ambulance the following week.

I will never forget the lovely Anosh. He had a horrid mouth cancer and was dying in an awful hard way. He was only in his 20s, and he had come to the Western from his ship docked on the Clyde. Anosh was an Iranian sailor and a very handsome one at that. He could hardly swallow anything but one thing he loved was coffee. I would make him some at night when the visitors were in.

He also got visitors, but it was during the day. The captain of his ship and about 8 Iranian sailors would come in to the ward looking so smart in their uniforms. I recall they had a red stripe on their caps, and all of them were so kind to Anosh and would ask me if he needed anything. I thought of Anosh's parents back in Iran not able to visit their dying son, and I gave him so much love from my heart and care during his end days. I can still see his face in my mind even today and telling you this makes me weep with sadness.

There was also what they called the outdoor room at the end of the corridor. It was for emergency patients that came in out of hours. They were mostly Epistaxis (nose bleeds) patients, and they could become quite serious if the bleeding continued for long and it was known years ago that deaths could occur from them. The junior doctor would work on his own along the corridor with those patients and a great mess was left behind as he would be too busy to clean up, I thought this a crazy situation, so had a chat with Dr. Mackinley that we could use the room next to the female ward as it was used for storing bottles, dressings, and other stuff.

It had a couch and chair in it and enough room for a doctor to work in. I moved some of the storage to the ward area, got paper towel for the couch, found a steriliser for instruments, and made the room able to treat emergencies. Most importantly, I informed all the doctors that they would have to tell a nurse when the room was being used, or the whole project would not work. I informed the nursing staff that they would be responsible for cleaning up after the doctor had been working there. I got a book that they signed when it was cleaned, and the first week in the new treatment room was a success. Dr. MacKinley and other doctors thanked me each day, and they were delighted with it.

My first weeks in the unit were going well and we worked like that for the next few years. Then one day I was asked if I wanted to apply for a sister's post at the ear, nose, and throat hospital in St. Vincent Street. I felt I was content where I was, but when I told Joe that night, he thought it would be a good idea as it would give me an immediate pay rise. So off I went for an interview to St. Vincent Street Hospital.

It was a red brick building with nine consultants, and each one of them proficient in their specialty. The sisters that worked there had been at least 40 years working in the wards. I was only 22 and still inexperienced in lots of things. I had gained a post registration certificate at the Queen Elizabeth Hospital Birmingham, as you needed two certificates to become a ward sister.

The interview was taxing. The matron, assistant matron, and a consultant I knew from the Western asked me umpteen questions on how to deal with different situations. I'm sure they must have known I was not a great academic, but it was with practical work that I shone. I knew how to think wide of the box, and how to organise people around me with different tasks. I'm sure that's what pulled the strings for me getting the job. I was sorry to leave the Western, but the job ahead seemed to be like a path I had to take.

Married life was trotting along. Joe worked in Barr and Stroud at Anniesland Cross doing technical work. They made periscopes for submarines during the war, and he also went to college to gain a certificate that gave him more opportunities in his work and gained an LRIC. Weekends if we were off work together was mainly seeing our parents, and on occasions the Cinema, or visiting friends for meals and chat.

One weekend I thought I really must try and have his mum and dad up for dinner, so out came the recipe books. I had only cooked at nursing college and domestic science at school so did not have much experience with it. My wee mum was never a cook. It was basic food and she never showed me how to make meals. This was not a fault of hers, it just never crossed her mind that it was something I may need to know. Anyway, the date was set. I decided on chicken with bacon on top, vegetables, potatoes, then followed by baked Alaska. I was then told that they would bring along their Aunt Jean and Uncle Angus. They were a really elderly couple.

I got everything ready. I had no baking tray for they food to cook in the oven, so improvised with covering each piece of chicken individually with tin foil (a brilliant idea I thought). In our kitchen then was a pull-down bed as they had years ago. After a short cooking time I began to feel extremely tired I had been working hard that week. I lay down on the bed to fall asleep, after some time Joe came into the kitchen to see how the meal was progressing (he was always one for good impressions). He shouted me awake, ran to open the windows and doors, and put off the gas oven.

It turned out the juice had spilled over on to the gas flames and extinguished them and I was slowly being gassed to death. Thankfully I was none the worse of the drama and the meal went down with a lot of compliments, especially the baked Alaska. Who would have thought to put ice cream in the oven? I served it with tinned fruit and pouring cream. The first meal was a great success and the start of many future cooking triumphs I had. I sound big headed here, but for me to cook a nice meal, that was a real achievement.

We were in the flat in Elie Street for 4 years, and then Joe suggested we bought a house suitable for a family with a garden and space for children to play if we had any. We put the flat on the market, and we bought it for £4,500 which was a lot then. Several couples came to view it, as the flat was handy for staff working in the hospital or university. It was valued at £6,000, and a guy came up to view it one day. He looked very trendy in his huge white platform boots, and he said he would be getting it and would put in a good offer. He was the highest bidder at £7,800 and we were over the moon. This gave us money for decent furniture for our new house. We ended up in Bishopbriggs just outside Glasgow.

Before we moved lots had to be done. Removal men were to come, and they said they would arrive the following day as we had a piano to move and they needed straps to carry it. This was a great excuse to take time off work I thought, and it was difficult being a nurse, so the following day was set.

The night before the move I thought of doing a small washing load in my twin tube washing machine that we had recently bought. I put it on and when rinsing the wash I forgot to put the out hose into the sink. I went through to watch John Cleese in Fawlty Towers on the TV. It had been such a laugh of a program, when I went through to the kitchen it was 4 inches deep in water. I ran about like Manuel in the program looking for trays to scoop the water up.

I worried the wee deaf lady downstairs may be flooded, so I rang the light up doorbell, and she looked puzzled. I ran to her kitchen and saw her ceiling was fine. There was a foam back carpet in the kitchen (not my idea). It was huge and we thought we could not leave it for the new guy, so at 10pm at night we folded and lifted the carpet downstairs. Every step gave out gallons of water all over the close, and it was like a *Carry On* Movie. The thing weighed a ton, and Joe had the bright idea to chuck it out the stair window. I said no as we could kill someone underneath with it, so all the way down two flights of stairs to the bin area we carried the carpet. Next morning I came down the stairs, the close window was still open from Joe's plan to chuck it out there. I looked down from the window outside, here was every telephone connection for all the flats. If we had chucked it out then half of the West End would have been cut off. The things you do when you are young and daft.

Holidays were few and far between, as the expense was too much for our meagre wages, so a camping trip was planned and Oban seemed the best place to visit. I felt that it was my real home, where I had relatives to see, boat trips to go on, and even a short flight to Mull.

The tents were borrowed from friends, camping equipment was cheap, food could be tins of beans, packets of dried food. This sounded more like a space mission than camping. I planned to take all my essential toiletries: shampoo, perfume, conditioner, body lotion, nail clippers, sun lotion, and everything that Boots the chemist provided me with.

I was told no, it would be too heavy to carry that lot, so just a bar of soap. How could I survive, I thought? Anyway, off we set on the train north to Oban Station. We walked to Ganavan Sands and pitched up the tent. The ground was hard as rock, and the tent was basic with no sealed ground sheets in those days. Bugs were all around us, especially the dreaded midgy that bites and sucks your blood. There were millions of them.

I made a dried packet of curry and it smelled delicious. We were both starving after our train journey and walk. Unfortunately, the frying pan tipped into the sand, and Joe took a hairy fit at me. We ate it all anyway, with all the crunchy bits of sand too.

The next day I took a walk into Oban to visit my aunt. As I walked along past the caravans parked near us I saw a familiar face. It was Tom the plumber from Hairmyres Hospital. He asked me to come and meet his wife and son. As I came to the door of his caravan, here was a little boy about two years old. It turned out I knew him as I had looked after him in the hospital. I never knew that Tom was his dad, and it was a chance meeting but a lovely moment in my life.

The weather was brilliant for our whole fortnight, and we travelled to Mull on a Loganair flight. The journey was hairy but exciting. It left from Connel Airport, if you could call it that. It was just a strip of ground for the plane to take off. We saw Lismore Light House, Duart Castle (the seat of the McLean Clan), the Isle of Mull, and surrounding islands. The views were spectacular, and we landed on a field in Glenforsa. It had a fire engine parked at the end of the field but nothing else. Jings, we were still alive I thought.

From there we hitched a lift to a village. An elderly couple stopped their car, and we put our bags in the boot and sat in the back seat. Before we knew it they began to argue. She was driving it a bit like Hyacinth Bucket and with poor Richard the husband. They ended up shouting at each other, but thankfully we got to our destination without murder.

I went into one of the hotels on the island and asked if I could have a bath. I explained that I was camping and had not had a decent wash for ages. The receptionist was so kind she gave me bath liquids, soap, towel, and said it was all free just go to the bathroom along the corridor. She was my angel from heaven I thought. People on the West Coast are always very kind and not at all money orientated. The bath was wonderful and I felt amazing getting all the dirt scrubbed away. Like Clint Eastwood after his desert walk having his bath in a hotel.

We got back to base in Oban and travelled down to Easdale where we camped on a hill near the hotel. When we woke up in the morning the tent was being attacked by a donkey. It was having a scratch on the tent cords and the tent nearly collapsed on top of us. That night we went to the hotel bar for a refreshment (a name given for drinking when it's just soft drinks). We were told that where we were camped was a piece of land owned by a local woman in the area. We were not in anyone's way so we moved on to find a better place.

Malaig further north sounded nice, so off we set on the West Highland line. The journey was spectacular with views of the West Coast mountains, the Glenfinnen Viaduct, Prince Charles' Statue, and all a painting for future.

We ended up in Morar, at a camping and caravan site on a sandy beach. There were all nationalities camped there: Germans, French, Americans, English, and I think we were the only Scots. After a night's sleep and some rainfall we started to organise breakfast on the small Calor stove. It was a nightmare as the Midgys were eating us alive. I went into my tent and put a stocking over my head. It made me look like a bank robber, but I didn't care as I wasn't getting any bites and could move around easily. The fellow campers all laughed loudly at me as did Joe. Few spoke English, but within a minute of two they all found a stocking for their heads. I had the last laugh, and one or two gave me the thumbs up sign which was comical.

I decided that camping was not for females with no proper wash, no cleaning clothes, bugs everywhere, no decent food, and no toilets for privacy. The first time I hid behind a bush for the loo a frog jumped between my legs. No, this was not my idea of fun, and I looked on it as an experience only.

To go back to my new job as ward sister was quite a thought, but another experience lay ahead.

My Friend's Wedding.

Scotland were playing football and the Scottish fans were clad in their usual mad tartan outfits. The train to London was packed full of wild, happy singing fans, and every one of them was full of excitement and alcohol. Sadly, Scotland played badly and lost 5-1 to England, so all that excitement was for nothing.

Joe and I sat in a quiet area on the train with some English business-people trying to avoid the crazy banter, and we were not given peace. Every so often a fan would scream into the compartment and shout an obscenity. I just laughed at their daftness, but the other passengers

97

were not amused at all. The guard threatened to throw a few off the train, but it was only a threat.

We were travelling to my friend Mary Sin Yan Too's wedding where she and fiancé Guy would marry at a church near Piccadilly. Mary arranged where we were staying, and it looked super from the outside with mock Tudor wood with white background. We were shown to a room in the attic. The guest house owner opened the door in front of us, and the smell of gas hit me in the face. I said, "Is that gas I'm smelling or is it my imagination?"

"It's your imagination," she replied. Whenever she disappeared, I went over to the gas fire, and it was on a peep. I opened the window and door to air the room after turning it off. I couldn't believe that we could both have died in our bed.

The next morning I asked the owner for a towel, and she handed me what looked like a duster. I declined the offer and dried myself in the bed sheet. When we went down for breakfast the other guests looked like they had just come off a dingy on the Channel. They were poor, sad looking families staring at us as we sat down. Breakfast was crumbly Cornflakes, and the end of the packet and nothing else. It was our own fault not to book ourselves. The lesson was never get anyone else to plan your stay. It was the 1970s and Hotels were for the well off. There were no Granadas then.

For the wedding I dressed in a Caftan (all the fashion of the day then). It was cream with flowers and I had sewn it myself. As we approached the church lots of friends were outside. Mary's brother Frank, cousins, aunts, and one of the bridesmaids who look worried were all there.

On either side of Mary were two small Chinese twin boys dressed in bow ties, and smart suits. Frank approached me and smiled saying, "Iona, the bridesmaid has nobody to look after her children, would you mind doing it for her?"

I offered to take on the two mischievous looking 3-year-olds (silly me). As I walked into the church with Joe I had a child in each of my hands with both pulling hard in opposite directions. It made the Caftan look like a floating aeroplane, and every head in the church turned looking in amazement probably wondering what are two Scottish people were doing with Chinese children.

We sat down and I told the boys they had to be very good and sit nice and quiet as Mary and Guy were getting married. To my horror the boys both scrambled under the seat in front and ran up to the alter where the priest, bride, and groom were being very serious and repeating their vows. Again heads turned to look around at us thinking and what awful "parents" we were. Then the boys went under the alter table, laughing and giggling. They ran around it several times, and I could feel my heart thumping. Just then an elderly woman grabbed the two of them and took them back beside her.

Trying to explain to folks at the reception that the boys were not ours was so embarrassing.

It was a beautiful wedding and Mary and Guy emigrated to Canada where they had two lovely girls. After many years of marriage Mary passed away recently. She was a dear friend whom I loved very much. A few years before I was happy to visit with her in her homeland the beautiful Mauritius, in the south east, off the tip of Africa. I met all her lovely family and was treated like a princess by her friends and relations.

I will never forget her wedding a happy funny day in my life.

CHAPTER 13

My beautiful Baby Boy.

We called him Scott. No other reason than just a name we both liked. They say you chose your name in heaven before you come to earth.

Although I had nursed and looked after lots of babies, to have your own is so different. I had only the knowledge I had learnt from college, The School of Nursing, and sadly not my mum. She lived in her own wee world and never taught me how to deal with childbirth or looking after a baby. Luckily, instinct kicks in and you muddle through.

Scott woke at 1 am that first night home, and Joe and I ran around the bedroom like headless chickens trying to keep him happy. I breast fed him, and don't know if you can say that now, but that's what it was. He was given a dry nappy and I tried unsuccessfully to settle him, and he screamed most of the night. I phoned the midwife in the morning, and she just told me to feed him. Unfortunately, this was to no avail as he was a colic baby, and cried most of his first few months until he got solid food.

My mother-in-law said he wasn't getting enough milk and nourishment with my breast milk, so I topped it up with bottle milk. If you see photos of Scott as a baby he was too heavy and fat. I was clueless like most mums for the first year, but he grew up strong and healthy.

Not long after Scott came Stuart, another 9 pound Baby. Born just 19 months after his brother in the Queen Mother's Hospital, he was a natural birth that was so pleasant and totally different from my first birth experience. He was long and with a huge head of black hair, and he slept most of the time. I had to waken him for feeds he slept so well, and they say if you could have your second child first you would know what to do.

Both boys were such great wee pals and they always played happily together.

Money was tight when I gave up ward work and no way did I want to put my babies into nursery for someone else to bring them up. I did it all myself with only once or twice asking my neighbor to babysit for me.

I decided to get night duty as a bank nurse. I could be put to any hospital in my area to work and the pay was £42 for a night's work. I worked at weekends while Joe babysat and his parents came out to help him. I slept until around 3 pm during the day and the awful feeling when I got home from the hospital after my shift made me feel like collapsing. However, needs must and when you have children it's amazing how you find that extra strength to carry on.

When not working I would have my mum, Anna, and Joe's parents out for a meal on Sundays. It was a lovely get together and some days I think it would be lovely to turn back the clock and have those happy times again.

The boys were growing and so were the bills. Mrs. Thatcher was Prime Minister at the time, and everyone was skint and we had great difficulty making ends meet. Money was pouring in for the rich and people were working for nothing. Wages were awful, and the country had strikes and we were at the end of our rope.

Then one day Joe phoned me from work and said he was offered a super job in New Hampshire, U.S.A. He was to be given a wonderful wage and title of Vice President of a branch of the company near Nashua, New Hampshire. This I thought was our passage out of living on the edge an I agreed on the phone and said, "Yes."

I had to appear at his work for an interview on how I felt about the new job. They probably were wondering how I would cope with two wee boys and a totally new environment.

The job was accepted and Joe went over ahead of me to find a place to stay temporarily for us, and also to get an office for the new work premises. All this was very exciting, and we decided to rent our home out until we were sure we would stay in America. Then it hit us how hard it would be for family and grandparents to pack up and go over the pond, but when you are young and trying to make your life better you tend to make decisions quickly without thinking wide of the box.

Flying then was the days before terrorists and the strict security at Airports. There was a sense of going on a long summer holiday and freedom to wander round the airport without hassle. The boys loved watching the planes take off and land, and there was viewing areas at Glasgow Airport and Heathrow where all the excitement could be seen.

It was a very long flight (10 hours) and really amounted to nearly a two-day travel time. The thoughts of saying a final goodbye to our family hurt me inside, but I had to think positive about it all for the sake of our wee family.

We arrived at Logan Airport and it was great to meet up with Joe again after those weeks apart, the boys kissed and hugged him and he made such a fuss over us all, it was such a happy moment.

We got to an apartment or condominium as it's called there. There was a pool, gym, tennis court, and sitting room for games. The flat was basic, very bachelor, but looked functional.

I got some sleep then unpacked our clothes. When our furniture arrived a few weeks later the flat started to look more homely, but that was before the awful crisis in our family.

Stuart was only two and a half when one night he started saying his throat was sore. He had a temperature, so I decided to sleep in his bed with him. At 5am I thought his breathing didn't sound right. I woke Joe and we all drove early morning to Nashua Memorial Hospital with a very sick wee boy. When we walked in with him, the doctors and nurses rushed him for X-ray telling me they would have to intubate him. They took him to a private room and I was to wait outside in the waiting area.

I could hear in the near distance Stuart crying as the medical staff tried to save his life. He had become quite cyanosed just before admission, but thankfully when they managed to put a tube down his nose and into his Airway his colour improved. The doctor explained that the fact the tube was down his nose meant he didn't need a tracheotomy. That was a relief I thought.

They whisked him to intensive care unit and he was given antibiotics and morphine intravenously. To see your child lying in that awful state broke my heart, and Joe was also upset but we had to be strong for Scott who was only three at the time. He kissed his brother on the cheek and told him to get well, and inside I was a wreck.

I stayed every day with him in ICU, and I only ate once or twice and that was at his bedside. After a couple of days, the doctor came in to speak to me, and he said he didn't know what was wrong with Stuart. He decided to phone Boston's Main Children's Hospital, and he spoke to a consultant about the situation. The doctor said they had sent a bacterial swab, and the consultant thought it was Epiglottis. This is an infection that causes the epiglottis to swell and block the airway. They changed Stuart's antibiotics and he began to progress slowly. His temperature came down, and his colour came back to cheerful pink and we sighed with great relief.

I decided to go home for a short while to have a wash and eat something. When I got back to the flat there was mail behind the door. It was bills for hundreds of dollars, at least twenty of them. They were for x-rays, blood tests, and bacteriology. Intensive care alone cost $1000 a day, and all to be paid quickly. In the wisdom of the company they never covered insurance for health. We had no clue that these things would be needed. It was not like today where you don't travel without health cover. Thankfully, the company paid the full costs of over $10000 dollars. This was a relief. In the end we sold our house back home in Scotland after not being able to find suitable tenants that would live in it. Students came to look at it, and another family with ten people. We thought it unfair to our neighbours to give them large groups of folk next door.

The day came for Stuart to have his tube removed after a week of treatment. He was to sit on my knee and I was to hold his head tight. I was also told that he could die if this did not go well.

My prayers are always answered from the great creator, so I closed my eyes and spoke to my maker. The tube slipped out without trouble. Stuart took a cough and cleared his throat, and I asked if I could take him to see the Christmas tree on the balcony. When he saw it he shouted, "Big tree mummy." It was a happy moment that sticks in my heart always, and he got home for Christmas Day.

He spoke to his grandparents on the phone, and we had only told them he had a sore throat. When he was so unwell it was a bit of a lie, but to tell them the truth would have upset them too much.

There is a marvelous part of this story I have kept until now and that was meeting two lovely ladies in Greeley Park, Nashua. A few days before Stuart was ill, I had taken the boys to the local park for swings. Two women were there, and one had two boys similar ages to mine. I didn't know a soul in New Hampshire, and so chatting with them was a joy.

One was a nurse from Canada, and the other was her friend. We all arranged to meet the following week, and needless to say because of Stuart being unwell I phoned to cancel our meet up. The day I got home from hospital for my wash and eat, Ann Vose, the nurse appeared at my door with a Shepherd's Pie. Her friend Judy Kenniser had made Cookies for us. Ann Phoned every night Stuart was in Hospital, and it was such a great support for me. She was an angel from heaven I thought. We are still in touch after so many years (40 years ago). At that I realised how great American and Canadian people were and so friendly. We saw each other every week during my stay in the states.

We moved to Merrimack, New Hampshire shortly after, and I still kept in touch with my friends there. I met other friends, Pat McPhee, and another friend after all these years, I'll speak of her later in my story.

I saw them most weeks. I didn't work at nursing in the states as the boys were still young and to pay for child care would have been futile it would have sucked up all my wages. I thought I will get back to work when Stuart's at school. Thinking back I had the idea to turn a part of my huge home with seven and a half acres of land into a garden centre come tearoom with restaurant, but it wasn't to be.

Joe asked for a pay rise and got double what he was getting. Ten thousand a year is a poor wage in America, and things began to look up. Although I was very homesick, a horrible feeling I may add, we were at last settling into American life.

Scott went on the yellow school bus for the first time, and he had been at a playgroup for a couple of hours a week. Stuart was stretching in height and becoming nearly the same height as his brother.

I was decorating the house slowly, and I laid a carpet in the family room. I sat down after being so pleased it turned out looking good. Then the rocking chair I was on caused the milk on my tray to spill all over it, and milk stinks when sour. I could have wept.

The snow came with bitter cold of negative 40 degrees below at times. I thought the first time I experienced it that a fly had gone up my nose, but it was just ice on my nasal hairs. The boys played making snowmen, ice slides, tunnels in the snow, and we had to dig ourselves out of the drive after a snowfall.

The house was toasty warm with wood burner and oil heating, but on occasions the water was cut off, and also the electric. I put casseroles on top of the wood stove and filled the bath with water. I had been through worse in Glasgow, so this was a doddle.

Ann Vose and her husband Richard from New York invited us to a barbecue and sledging day. We all arrived at this huge hill, climbing to the top in our boots and cosy jackets. He had made a massive sledge to hold all of us. The boys and other kids were in the middle, the men at the front and back, and the ladies either side of the kids. Richy shouted down the hill for other sledgers to move aside, and then we all slid down the hill at what felt like seventy miles an hour. I've never been a scaredy cat, but that was terrifying and daft I thought. Never again I felt, as we could all have had broken bones, head injuries--the lot. Gosh, it was some ride.

Christmas was hard being away from home, but we all spoke on the phone, so it was nice hearing our folks on the other end.

All our Family came over on holidays, although it was an expense for them. Anna stayed two weeks and hated the bugs and snakes in our yard. She took ages to dress in the morning, and it was 11am before the day began with the boys chomping at the bit to get out.

One day she put on an all-white outfit, and we walked round the area and she sat on a seat. It turned out it was wet paint, and the sign had blown off. Her outfit was covered in brown paint. We went to a store and the guy who served us was great. He gave us a lotion, not turps, but it took every drop of paint out of the white clothes. I was amazed and happy it worked a treat.

Life trotted on and I was kept busy with decorating and housework, and seeing to meals. In summer they were cooked on the barbecue as it was so hot inside. We didn't have air conditioning back then.

We met nice people and my neighbours made us so welcome. We were asked to a dinner and dance by a couple, and I phoned Nancy who gave us the invite. I told her in the UK dinner and dances were very formal with long dresses for ladies and bow ties and suits for men. I asked her what sort of outfit to wear, and she replied, "Oh, just whatever you want, anything goes."

I searched my clothes to find a bright cerise pink blouse and navy floaty skirt with glitter thread through it, sparkly shoes, and pink tights to match-- just the job I thought. When I walked through the door of the hall where the dance was, I could see a stare from those around me. It turned out it was a Elk's Dance for charity, and everyone was in red elk t-shirts with jeans. Here was Cinderella looking like a spare. I enjoyed the night and everyone complimented my attire to my embarrassment.

What to wear in America was hard for me to adjust. I sent the boys to Sunday School and when I went to collect them, all the kids had track suits on. he boys had shirts, ties, smart grey trousers, and leather shoes. Scott said to me on the way out, "Mum, maybe we should wear casual next week."

"Yes son", I answered.

In Scotland church is for seeing God in your very best clothes. We had a laugh about it.

At another time it was Christmas and we were asked to neighbour's house. I thought I'd better dress down. I got there in my plain cotton dress, and everyone wore long velvet dresses and suits. The next time I'll go out in fancy dress I thought if anyone invites me to dinner.

Americans were a bit like the Glasgow people. They were very friendly, chatty, and full of joy to speak to. They were all interested in my accent. I visited Boston each week to the museums and Marine Centre. The boys loved seeing it all, and we went a tall building to the top of the world, with the lift rushing up leaving my stomach behind. Everywhere was great, but driving was not so great. I managed to navigate most places without a map or sat nav which were not around then.

We returned to Scotland for Anna and Alastair's wedding. Alistair was a lovely man whose folks were from Harris. He like me was brought up in Glasgow.

I was maid of honour, and dressed like a blancmange in a huge pink dress. My skinny days were over after eating American food. Seeing all the family again was terrific, a sad and happy feeling I would say. Anna was a most beautiful bride and got married in the free church in Glasgow. Her cleavage was hidden for the service with a large white rose. The boys wore kilts with sporrans and with photos taken everywhere. Another happy moment.

CHAPTER 14

Life's Teaching.

Some people have died and come back to life. I mentioned this previously, and with modern medicine and ways to revive those who have collapsed and died, they sometimes have what is known as an NDE (Near Death Experience). I can honestly say that none of my patients told me of this when they were resuscitated. I had only one strange happening when working in high dependency in The Aberdeen Royal Infirmary. I never told anyone about it afterwards, as people tend to think it's imagination when these things occur, but this was very real. I was working one day checking my patients who had been through huge operations. I went into a lady's room to check her recordings, and she was not breathing. She was blue in colour, and as I ran out the room to get the doctor I heard her voice come from the top corner of the ceiling, say "I'm alright nurse, don't worry." I knew it was her voice as she had a husky rough sound always when she spoke. I quickly turned round, but she was still very dead. We tried to bring her back, but to no avail. It was such a poignant moment and I have remembered it clearly all these years.

There are lots of these NDE stories on YouTube that are so interesting, especially Nanci Danison', a top American lawyer who had an experience of death during an operation.

These people come back from death with fascinating stories of what they have learned of why we are here as humans on earth. One of the things they say are that we want to test ourselves and learn how to love and forgive. These two things are so important to our inner souls, and we plan what we are going to do on earth when in heaven, like a play on stage. Earth is our stage for acting out what we feel as reality, and the actors all decide who is going to play what role, who is going to go through the hurt or joy, but it is all learning for our soul.

My learning was very traumatic, hurtful, devastating, and shattering to my life, but importantly I have forgiven the culprits and look on them that they have taught me a wonderful lesson.

The story begins when Joe was doing extra work and travelling to trips in the UK and other places. He was away for a few weeks at a time, and when home he seemed depressed and upset. I put it down to overwork. I had to renew my passport at this time so thought to go to New York where there was a British Embassy was. I didn't know about sending it through the post, and I don't think you could do that then. I decided to turn it into a holiday and go to Ottawa in Canada for my passport renewal.

I took the Boys with me. As I drove into Montreal I noticed all the road signs were in French, not a language I spoke as I said earlier. As it was getting dark I thought it wise to check into a hotel to be safe for the night. The reception was staffed with a guy who was French standing with a vest on that Paw Brown would be proud of. Not being snobby, I still thought it best to stay here, rather than driving around some strange new city.

Another staff member came out and helped me book in. Thankfully, she was English speaking. I took the boys to the same room as me, pulled the chest of drawers in front of the door, and we all eventually slept after much racket from the corridor. I think it was a bonking hotel. The bath water in the morning was black, and obviously never used. It was a ridiculous experience and when light came we all got on with our journey.

I got to Ottawa after a fair drive, and the boys used an empty milk carton for wee wees, and to save stopping in strange places. Ottawa was a beautiful city, with green topped buildings and lots of sunshine that day. We decided to go to the park across the road from the embassy for lunch as it wasn't opened until one-thirty. Typical British--everything stops for food.

The park was full of working people: nuns in white habits, men in smart suits, and all eating their food. We sat by a fountain and munched on some sandwiches bought at a nearby stand. The boys asked afterwards if they could have a paddle, as it was so hot so I thought, "Go for it guys," Paddle meant being just splashing their feet in the water. At that they both jumped up to their waists in water, and people round the fountain gasped in horror. I had to pull them out and take them back to the car for a clothes change. We walked into the embassy with me looking smart, and the boys with wet hair looking like two drowned mice.

I got the new passport no bother, and we continued our drive visiting Niagra Falls. It was an amazing sight to see. Scott said when he saw it, "Is this it mum?" He had recently seen the Superman film with action, helicopters, and excitement--hence his disappointment. We journeyed on, driving for miles, and eventually we all got home safely. Joe looked shocked to see us back early, and he thought we would be away longer. "No, here we are,'" I said.

When out in the garden with Stuart the next day, a huge rattlesnake appeared. There were snakes all over the area, but not rattlers. We froze on the spot, and I got Stuart to walk back very slowly, and then we both ran into the house as fast as we could. Looking back maybe it was a bad omen to see such a scary thing, as something was about to happen.

A few weeks later I got a phone call from Joe saying he would be home later, and he was just going to meet up with some work colleagues, and he would be home around 7pm. Seven o'clock came and went and another phone call from him saying he was eating in the Manyana, a Restaurant two miles down the road from our house.

I came off the phone. It was 9pm and the boys were sleeping in bed. I thought this is not on, so I got the boys into the car, got some oven gloves, and grabbed the fish casserole I had made him,. I drove to the restaurant and walked in past the startled waiters. My heart sank. There in front of me was Joe with a woman at a table, I put the fish dish down in front of him and said, "Here is your meal. You can eat it here or at home." I then turned to the woman and said, "Excuse me," and walked out in disgust.

He could have come home and told me it was a work colleague and told me off for causing an embarrassing moment, but he came clean and poured out his extra marital affair that had been going on for a year. I had smashed our lovely wedding photo from the top of the piano at the front door for him to climb over when he came home. This maybe made him speak the truth for once.

He had talked of putting our house up for sale before all this happened, and the plan was I would go back home. He would tie up things here and I would follow on later. I now saw clearly what his masterplan was. Estate Agents came to the House, saying how cute it was to see British decor.

I had to make arrangements where to stay when back in the UK. My Sister and brother in-law were marvelous, although so shocked when I told them what had happened. Joe's parents were devastated completely when he told them what had happened to our family. My heart went out to them. They were such good living people in a respectable area of Glasgow who would be ashamed of what happened to their son's mind and this awful thing happening to us all. It never stopped me visiting them with the children when I got back to Scotland.

My friends and neighbours embraced me in my sorrow and were such excellent support to me. Some had husbands who had affairs and they were back together happily. It was amazing to hear of people's skeletons in cupboards, and it seemed a common occurrence. In Scotland nobody got divorced in those days. It was a shocking thing to happen and only a hundred years previously it was never permitted. There was a way for men to sort out their situation back then. They put their wives into mental asylums, or private houses to be looked after, then carried on with their lives and new lover. I suppose I was lucky if you could call it that.

I got a lot of support with a dear friend Pat McPhee who stayed in Amherst at the time. We would meet up every week and chat about everything. It must have been difficult for my friends to understand what was happening to Joe and I. They knew both of us so I'm sure didn't want to take sides and bring the other down. The change from respectable married couple to broken marriage was still looked on with revulsion then, especially if there were children involved.

Pat was a get up and go type of person. Her calendar was always full to the hilt with activities for her two children, and it made me feel lazy to hear what she was up to each week. At that time I didn't paint, read books, or socialise much. I just concentrated my energy on the kids and keeping them happy and entertained.

Pat's husband Sandy came over to visit me one day, and he advised me to stay in America. He said if I went back to Scotland I would lose

Joe. I could not think of staying, I felt I needed to be home with my family and the children's grandparents for support.

It's a lonely world when something like a marriage breakup happens. People don't like to interfere and tend to give you a wide berth and are probably embarrassed to come and visit you knowing how upset you will be. Some folk just can't take the drama I suppose.

The house sale went through. Joe with his lawyer and I with mine. The buyers were a couple with family, and umpteen other folk were round a large table. I felt this can not be happening to me and my kids.

I had to accept that Joe loved this woman and no force in the world would change that. I suppose I respected their wishes and bowed in the end not to make a fuss or lower myself to do anything daft. I had to keep sane for the sake of my boys. Love is a very strange thing sometimes, a huge force from the universe. We must follow it whatever.

My lawyer, a lady, began to speak. She tore into the legal side of things and began to say what would happen, and saying how her client would demand this and that.

"Stop the bus," I said. "Before we go any further, this will be an amicable parting and dividing of our property. My husband and I will decide what goes where, who gets what, and how often he will see his boys." Everyone sat in amazement listening to my words, as usually in America each partner tries to get as much as they can from a separation situation. It wasn't divorce yet, and I wanted to give Joe time to come to his senses.

I was lucky and came out well from it all. I got enough to get a house deposit back in UK, and also some of dollars for childcare, and what I want from the furnishings. I gave him all the electric goods, as they were of no use back in Glasgow having different voltage. He got the majority of photos as I thought he didn't have the boys with him, so the photos would be his. He could have what he wanted, which wasn't much. He got a sum of money, also enough for a deposit on a house, It all went as smoothly as these things could. We arranged for a removal company to take my stuff home to Scotland.

Then he told me that the company had sacked him for untruthfulness. I wondered if it was due to the fact that the company owner was married to a staff nurse that I worked with in the Western Infirmary. I arranged flights for the boys and myself.

The removal men arrived to pack our things, and they seemed to disappear every so often. I bought them all a meal at Burger King, and I drove the two miles to get it for them. I saw them take out what looked like a mattress box that seemed light but rattled a lot. I sniffed a rat, and I felt they were stealing from me. My Glasgow upbringing knows a thief when I see it.

I was right, when I opened the boxes when in my new home, the stuff had been flung I like rubbish, with cigarette burns on my furniture, Royal Doulton China flung in like junk, and they had not even wrapped the boy's toys. Half the things were stolen, with Swiss Army Knives Joe had brought as gifts for us all from his Swiss trip years before. To lose your home, your marriage, your American friends, and security was bad enough, but this topped it all. How could these people do such a rotten thing? It's their karma, not mine.

I said goodbye to my friends, I paid the final bills on the house, and closed bank accounts in the states. Joe saw us to New York Kennedy Airport, and he cried like a baby saying his goodbyes. I kept my composure for the sake of the boys. It was a long flight, and we were all exhausted.

The flight up to Glasgow from Heathrow was difficult. I had to have Stuart on my knee, and Scott sat across from me next to a business-man. Scott started to feel sick, and I asked the guy to hold the paper bag under his chin. The stewardesses were strapped in for the takeoff, and the poor guy looked as sick as Scott when he helped him vomit into the bag.

I thanked him kindly and handed the bag to the staff later. It was upsetting for my children as much as myself. I had explained to them that daddy wasn't coming home with us, and that he found another lady he loved. He still loved them but had to stay with her in America. Maybe it was too harsh for them to understand, but I felt they had to know I wasn't running away from their dad and that Joe still Loved them.

Joe got to have the boys for summer holidays for 6 weeks. He could see them any time he wanted, and they were his as much as mine. He still loved them dearly, but also loved his new lady. She had a daughter

Alison, who was still very young. It must have been such a shock for her to discover her mum had a new partner. Today Alison and I are good friends, and I have been to her house and met her family. She is a very special person..

I was obviously devastated about it all but had to stay strong for the boys. I said my prayers and moved on with my life. For a long time I woke each morning crying to myself, and the awful hurt was still very raw. I wasn't crying for me, but for the children without a dad. Scott also cried a lot as he was only 6 yrs. old. Stuart, 4, kept his feelings to himself. In later years I discovered he remembered the casserole incident.

We stayed with Anna and Alistair for 3 Months, and it was a squash for them. They insisted I got their bed, and the boys slept on the living room floor in sleeping bags. Anna and Alistair slept in a tiny pull-down settee. Meanwhile I house searched in Bishopbriggs, and I found a place quickly. I think I bought it for the lovely garden, but the house needed renovating big time.

Everyday since I had got the house, I went out to Bishopbriggs to decorate. Not to sound boastful, but I was pretty good at it. I asked my cousins and Joes friend Ian if they would help, Anna and Alistair also did a lot of work for me. The kitchen was tiny but adequate for our needs. I measured its size, and left a couple of inches for each side of white goods. We went down to Comet on Byers Road and ordered a washing machine, dishwasher, dryer, cooker, and more. The joiner came to fit units I had ordered, and he said I got a fitted kitchen for cheap with what I had done.

The electrician rewired the whole house, and he was brilliant--another angel from heaven. He helped me lift the old carpets and nine layers of flooring in the kitchen before decorating it, and he put all the junk in his van and took it to the tip.

I had the house now looking like new. The house was ready for the boys starting school in August. Poor Scott had to start from Primary One as the headmaster thought it best. This ended up an advantage to him, and he did well at school and so did his brother.

The headmaster was a hoot, and I went to see him to enroll the boys when I moved to the new house. He was helpful and assured me they would enjoy the school. He then said, "I was not to worry about them, and that children are little animals that just need some training." I was amused by his remark. My boys were little gentlemen I thought. I had trained them with good manners, to dress smartly, to take a pride in things, to respect others, to let elderly go through a door first. Not to kill, not to steal, and they went to Sunday School to learn right from wrong. This was all what my own parents and their parents had taught them. Animals indeed (NOT).

The lack of a father figure at home can sometimes wreck children's lives. They miss the male playing of football, the days out with dad to the cinema, and the laughs and jokes that men have with their boys.

All the dad stuff that women find hard to do is a challenge, such as fixing broken stuff in the house and lots more. Scott and Stuart had double the amount of love from me and they knew it. We had hugs, kisses before going out to school, pocket money. Scott spent some of his money on sweets for me. A bag of Liquorice Allsorts was handed to me after their visit to the shops, and they showed kindness abundant to me and I to them.

They saw their dad when he came over from the states, and they knew I still loved him. Scott saw me weep one night and he knew why as he had done the same. He put his arm around me and said, "Don't cry mum, you will be alright, I'll look after you always." My heart melted at his words, and it made me giggle at his words aged 7 yrs. He was the man of the house I told him. One morning he made me a cup of tea and gave me toast in bed. It was a special moment and the bond the three of us had was stronger than anything on earth.

They joined the junior Boy's Brigade, the Anchor Boys, and we went for a meal every month to a restaurant. I could not afford to take them on holidays, but they had 6 weeks with their dad in America, who by this time he had moved to the Chicago area.

They were given the run of the house, except the living room. It was only when I was in it that they were allowed to play there. I didn't want any more furniture damaged after my removal experience. We ate breakfast at the table together. I would cook eggs, bacon, and sausages on occasion. Fresh orange juice and milk was had every day, and they never wanted for home comforts and they helped me load the dishwasher and do small chores.

I read to them every night from Ronald Dahl Books. Charlie and the Chocolate Factory was a favourite, I gave them haircuts myself to save money, but not like the ones my dad had given me thankfully. We saw their grandparents nearly every week, and they had aunts and uncles of mine to visit too. We trotted on with our lives without Joe around, but phone calls were often to their Dad.

CHAPTER 15

Grandparents and Work.

Mr. and Mrs. Mueller stayed in Esmond Street, just across from the Glasgow Sick Children's Hospital and the Maternity Hospital where Stuart was born. It was on a hill, a big red sandstone building. Their house was pristine clean and Mrs. Mueller was so house proud. She would iron everything in sight, even the Cat if she had one. I would go up to see the boys and such a fuss was made over them. Mr. Mueller loved to see them, and he would chat away telling them his childhood stories. I sometimes brought a fish supper up for us all to eat, or Mrs. Mueller would cook a super meal for us all. They looked on me as a daughter, and they also felt the loss of their son, but we never spoke of that in front of the boys.

I had been 2 years on my own by this time, and Joe always asked me for a divorce. I thought I can't live my life in limbo, and I have to move forward, so I agreed to his request. I went to see his parents on the Sunday after this decision. By the Wednesday Mr. Mueller had had a massive stroke, and he was admitted to Gartnavel Hospital where he lay in a coma so very ill. I asked him to squeeze my hand once for yes and twice for no, and he did this. Mrs Mueller was able to have some kind of communication with him, and she didn't move from his bedside, except only for the toilet.

He died a couple of days later of a further stroke. She was devastated, and it was so upsetting for her to deal with. Joe came over to help make funeral arrangements. I kept my distance not to interfere, and I did visit her but not when he was around her. It was their private time I felt. She came home from the hospital exhausted. I helped her undress for bed, and my heart was sore for her loss. I felt if I had not announced the divorce to them, he would still be here, but God had another plan it seemed.

A few weeks after I was over visiting Anna and Alistair, I was sitting after work on their settee. Stuart ran over to cuddle into me and as I raised my right arm to hold him I felt a horrible pain over my breast area. I never let on to anyone at the time, but upon getting home I got into my nighty and felt what seemed like a two inch lump over my right breast. My heart sank. I didn't think of me and what I might have to go through. It was more of who would look after my boys.

The next day I made an appointment to see the GP, and he referred me to the hospital outpatients where a young doctor stuck a huge needle into my breast trying to aspirate fluid from it, to no avail. He said I would need an operation and quickly.

I arranged for Anna to look after the boys and went into the general surgery ward of the Western Infirmary. The doctor had booked me into my own training hospital.

There I met about six other ladies of various ages all with breast lumps. We all spoke of our lives and loves and supported each other for surgery the next day. Unknown to me one of them was Ian's (Joe's friend at school) Aunt. I didn't discover this till I was home.

We all wished each other good luck and the following day I signed a consent for possible total right mastectomy. My thoughts were never fear, but more irritation that I was in the middle of decorating my new house and this was such a hold up on it. Anna was to watch over the workmen in the house. Gardeners, electricians, plumbers, and plasterers. Things had to keep going, and the boys needed a nice home to come back to after school.

I came around from the anesthetic felling groggy and being pushed on a trolley through the ward. I was aware of patients all clapping loudly as I entered. I was wondering why? One of the ladies came up to me and said, "Congratulations, you still have your two boobs." I looked at my chest area and sure enough both were there in full sight. What a relief. It turned out it was just a benign tumour that had been removed causing only a tiny one-inch scar. I didn't need chemotherapy, radiotherapy, or mastectomy. I felt elated at that thought and grateful to all the hospital staff.

During my stay in hospital, Anna phoned me and said that the gardeners wanted more money for the job. They knew I was in hospital, so I felt they were taking advantage of my situation. I spoke to one of them and said we agreed on a price. He will have to do the job with that payment and not a penny more. He went off in the huff but did as I said.

When arriving back home I looked up at the plaster work, and there were lumps all over it. It was a bad job, and a rushed no doubt. He had also flung plaster all over my white machines in the kitchen. I thought what creep to do work like that. Anna had paid him and off he had gone. There was no receipt, and no way was I wanting to argue with him after my hospital experience. I was just glad to be back home again, even though it was messy.

A few months after all that and it was spring and Scott had lost the key to the hut where he kept his bike. I got the ladder and screwdriver out and removed the hinges, and as I lifted the door from the hinges it fell on my right toe. It was not painful at the time. I took his bike out, screwed the hinges back on, carried the ladder down to the house, and then the ghastly pain in my toe hit me.

I felt faint so told Scott to get my neighbour in case I fainted. I lay in bed feeling agony. In came my neighbour, and she moved my toe wiggling it right and left, saying I don't think it's broken. I knew it was with the pain.

I phoned Anna and she watched the boys as I went to x-ray department at Stobhill.

"Oh yes," said the Doctor. "You have a broken big toe, but we can't see to it today. It was Friday, and there were no staff that could plaster it for me. I had to return on Monday, and Alistair kindly gave me a lift to the orthopedic area. He waited in the car for my return, and low and behold I had a cast up to my knee with crutches to help me walk. Alistair's face turned white when he saw me, as he was never one for the sight of injuries. The next few weeks were hard, hopping around like a grasshopper on one foot in the house. What next I thought.

I went to the dentist one day, and he was quite a chatty friendly man who gave me a filling no bother. He asked what my type of work was, and I told him I was a nurse but had just returned from America after a short stay. He asked if I was trained, and I told him I was state registered. "Just what I'm looking for," he said. He was opening a new nursing home in Airdrie called Arran house, and it was previously a home for nuns. He said he needed a matron for it, and I agreed to take up the post. This would be good for me to find work and get me back to helping people again.

The day was set for starting, and after another short interview with the administrator I went to get a uniform for the job ahead. We organised beds, basins, chairs, first aid boxes, and all the things required to look after elderly people in a nursing home. The planning was vast, and the boss was great at getting things done. We visited a friend of his who had a home in Ayr. She was up and running for a few years, and we got some tips on staffing levels and what equipment was needed for our new premises.

I booked the boys into after school care, and it would only be for a couple of hours. I didn't want to give them a door key like I had aged 8 in Glasgow. It was a different world from then, so I felt they needed somewhere for after school. A neighbour took them for 15 mins every morning as I left Bishopbriggs at 8.15am for my work. They were kind and didn't take payment.

The painters came into the nursing home and painted everything in sight except me. It was dark brown wood was sparkling white. The dreary rooms were covered in floral wallpaper, and I thought they would have been better painted walls, but no. Wallpaper all around each room.

The staff were interviewed by the boss, the administrator, and myself. We interviewed local people. One girl who was very bonnie looking and made both the men excited about her joining our team. I phoned to see if she was on the nurse register. She wasn't, and she had lied to us at the interview.

I phoned her to say she was unsuccessful in her job application. Her mum phoned me an hour later, calling me all the names under the sun, but I didn't give in. The men were disappointed. You have to be careful who to employ in a nursing home, as the elderly residents were extremely vulnerable.

The nursing staff that came to work with us were the best, and all great workers and all good at their job. I mostly gave out the medicines and tried to help with the bathing of residents. I also helped the residents in their everyday living.

One day the cook walked out after somebody complained about his brown gravy. He was a good cook, but this left a huge problem. Who would cook the rest of the meals? The boss was in a panic. "We can't give them Chinese or Indian take away. They will have Diarrhea the next day," he said. "I'll cook ," I answered. "Yes me, I can cook, if I get help."

I went down to the kitchen. The beef was all ready to serve, and I just had to make gravy for 42 residents, and some potatoes. I learned tricks on cooking in America, and so I washed the potatoes, sliced them thin, and covered them in oil. Then I put them in the oven and cooked them for 25 mins. I made rice pudding with raisins. I made the mistake of serving it cold. It came back to the kitchen for heating and went down a treat with the oldies. The meal was a success, and the day was saved.

We interviewed for another cook quickly. I went home and prepared cakes, apple pie, lemon pie, and more for next day's sweet. I made steak pie with carrots and mashed potatoes followed by a trolly filled with sweet cakes and pies. Another success thankfully. A cook was found and the day saved. Another event in the nursing home, and one of many.

It was winter and the snow fell deep over all over Glasgow. Everything in Scotland comes to a complete halt if it snows. The trouble is there are cars parked on roadsides all through the built up areas, so there is no room for snow ploughs to clear it all away. In America you could be fined for parking of the road if it snowed, and that way the roads were clear to drive on always even after 6 foot high snowfalls.

I arrived on time at the nursing home through heavy snow and slush over the roads. It was treacherous and very cold weather. There was a panic from the boss. The dip stick for the oil tank was read wrongly by the handyman, and consequently we had no oil in the tank. The boss quickly phoned and hired Calor gas heaters for the main living areas. Oil was ordered, but when they came to deliver it the tanker couldn't get up the sloping drive for snow. I phoned the local Airdrie Council and explained our dilemma. Thankfully they were out clearing the drive within half an hour, and the day was saved. This was after much worry and concern for the elderly residents who could have very quickly gotten hypothermia and worse.

I enjoyed my job immensely at the nursing home, but then I met a lovely man and my life changed again, big time. I had been on my own with the boys for two years at this point, and a dear friend phoned me and invited me to a dinner and dance in Edinburgh. I wasn't keen to go, but felt I was turning into a recluse with living in my little cocoon of just work and no social life at all. It was not the real me. I loved people's company and chatting to friends, but to go to functions with my past friends was hard. They were all with husbands and did everything with them. I felt intrusive in their lives, and I also felt they maybe thought with me being single I was a threat to their Marriage, so I lived in my own lonely wee world and was still tearful after two years.

To lose someone the way I had was like a death. That's the only way to describe it, and you grieve for your loss. A friend phoned me and asked if I would go to a dinner and dance with him. I was reluctant at first, then thought maybe it will cheer me up.

I dressed smart and walked in with my friend to meet a row of men all shaking hands with me. One of them shook my hand as though he was scared to touch me, and he only gave me the tips of his fingers when I held his hand. Something gave me a huge feeling of sadness for him, and I thought he had something in his life that hurt him a lot and it was a very strange moment.

I then discovered that my friend had announced to his colleagues that we would both be sharing a room upstairs in the hotel. I was mortified, and to think all those people thought of me like a Tart. It was probably my fault, and when he phoned to ask what kind of room he should book in the Hotel, I had mentioned that I like a double bed since I liked to stretch at night. I was not thinking for a minute that I meant him to join me. Another idiot moment of mine.

The dance began and I felt uncomfortable for most of the time but was trying to put on a good face. Then my eye caught the guy with the funny handshake. He looked so smart and clean, and I couldn't keep my eyes off him. I tried to look away from his gaze, but to no avail. He fascinated me when darting here and there chatting to everyone.

Then he asked me up for a dance. He whisked me off my feet once or twice, and I felt magical in his arms and he chatted away to me all the time. At the end of the night he gave me his phone number. I was still annoyed at my friend and gave him his bag from my car, before telling him to make his own way home next day. I was leaving I said.

It's the most awful thing I have ever done to anyone in my life and I will never forgive myself for treating him like that. I was so upset, not really about my friend, but more about my situation. He was being kind and I was behaving like a nut to him. I am still in touch with him and thinking back I loved him dearly, and still do, but God had another plan for my life.

CHAPTER 16

The Wedding

Scotland was playing football, and the Scottish fans were clad in their usual mad tartan outfits. The train to London was packed full with wild, happy, singing fans, each of them full of excitement and alcohol. Sadly, Scotland played badly and lost 5-1 to England, all that excitement for nothing.

Jim and I sat in a quiet area on the train with some English business people, trying to avoid the crazy banter. We were not given peace; every so often, a fan would scream into the compartment and shout some obscenity. I just laughed at their daftness, but the other passengers were not amused at all. The guard threatened to throw a few off the train, but it was only a threat.

We were travelling to my friend Mary Sin Yan Too's (Marie) wedding, where she and her fiancé, Guy, would marry at a church near Piccadilly. Mary arranged where we were staying, and it looked superb from the outside, mock Tudor wood with a white background. We were shown to a room in the attic. When the guest house owner opened the door, the smell of gas hit me in the face. I said, "Is that gas I'm smelling or my imagination?"

"It's your imagination," she replied. Whenever she disappeared, I went over to the gas fire, which was on a peep. I opened the window and door to air the room after turning it off. I couldn't believe that we could both have died in our bed. The next morning, I asked her for a towel. She handed me what looked like a duster. I declined the offer and dried myself with the bed sheet. When we went down for breakfast, the other guests looked like they had just come off a dinghy on the Channel, poor, sad-looking families staring at us as we sat down. Breakfast was crumbly cornflakes, the end of the packet, nothing else.

It was our own fault for not booking ourselves; lesson learned, never get anyone else to plan your stay. It was the 1970s, and hotels were for the well-off, no Granadas then.

I dressed in a caftan (all the fashion of the day), which was cream with flowers, and I had sewn it myself. As we approached the church, lots of friends were outside: Mary's brother Frank, cousins, aunts, and one of the bridesmaids, who looked worried. On either side of her were two small Chinese twin boys dressed in bow ties and smart suits. Frank approached me and smiled, saying, "Iona, the bridesmaid, has nobody to look after her children. Would you mind doing it for her?" I offered to take on the two mischievous-looking 3-year-olds, silly me. As I walked into the church with Jim and a child in each of my hands, both pulling hard in opposite directions, making the caftan look like a floating airplane, every head in the church turned, probably thinking, "What are two Scottish people doing with Chinese children?" We sat down. I told the boys they had to be very good and sit nice and quiet as Mary and Guy were getting married. To my horror, the boys both scrambled under the seat in front and ran up to the altar, where the priest, bride, and groom were being very serious and repeating their vows. Again, heads turned to look round at us, thinking what awful parents we were. Then the boys were under the altar table, laughing and giggling, running around it several times. I could feel my heart thumping. Just then, an elderly woman grabbed the two of them and took them back beside her. Trying to explain to folks at the reception that the boys were not ours was so embarrassing.

It was a beautiful wedding. Mary and Guy emigrated to Canada, where they had two lovely girls. After many years of marriage, Mary passed away recently, a dear friend whom I loved very much.

A few years before, I was happy to visit with her in her homeland, the beautiful Mauritius, southeast off the tip of Africa. I met all her lovely family and was treated like a princess by her friends and relations.

I will never forget her wedding, a happy, funny day in my life.

Nurse Peters Western Infirmary. Nurse Peters was an elderly lady who worked as a Staff Nurse on Night Duty at Western Infirmary. She was nearing retirement in a few months and was known for her meticulous morning reports, which included even the smallest details about her patients. On New Year's Eve, after finishing her evening shift, the Sister on the back shift came to me with instructions that there was a bottle of Sherry locked in the medicine cabinet and that the night nurses were allowed to have a small glass each for bringing in the new year. I handed the medicine keys to Nurse Peters and went home, but the next morning when I arrived for duty at 8 am, there was no sign of her. I enquired from the auxiliary nurse about her whereabouts and was told that she had been fired on the spot after being caught drunk and making inappropriate advances towards the night superintendent. This incident caused her to lose her pension and reputation. I felt deeply saddened by the loss of such a great nurse and the impact it had on the patients at Western Infirmary. It is always important to be mindful of the struggles that nurses and other healthcare workers face, and to offer support and resources when needed.

The Funeral

It was March in Glasgow, cold, wet, dark, and miserable. Mrs. Robertson had died on the 5th of the month. She was George's mum and a fine wee lady, always smiling, always generous, always helpful in every way. Every Sunday night, we would visit Mrs. Robertson and George in their room and kitchen on Kelvinhaugh Street. They had a color television, a novelty at the time, as nobody else we knew had one. The excitement of seeing everything in color was marvelous, a stark contrast to the black and white we were used to.

Tea and chocolate biscuits were served halfway through the program we watched. It was a lovely evening of entertainment and laughs.

I drove to Maryhill Crematorium Glasgow on the day of Mrs. Robertson's funeral. Everyone had met earlier for a short service at Argyll Street Funeral Directors. The crematorium was busy with a lot of mourners present. She had been well-known and popular, and it was sad to meet some old friends I hadn't seen for some 30 years. The minister gave a lovely speech and told the story of Mrs. Robertson's life in Glasgow. We all listened to hear about how she had worked in a sweet shop, how she had lost her husband early in her marriage, and how she had coped as a single parent with her son George to support. Although there was formality about the service, members of the congregation also spoke out and shared lovely stories. Everyone felt sad, especially for George, as his mum's coffin was lowered out of sight, its purple velvet cover becoming level with the surroundings. Heaven had just opened its doors to a wonderful person.

After the usual chats outside the church area, we were all invited to the Jury Hotel on Great Western Road, once known as the Pond Hotel when I worked at Gartnavel Hospital behind it some years earlier. We were shown to a room along the corridor set for a meal with two round tables. Only one table was needed, as many people had work to return to and some people shy away from these sorts of events. Twelve people sat down to eat, the round table making the gathering more friendly and conducive to chatting with each other.

The waitress appeared; she was very young, maybe 17, I thought, slim, dressed in the usual white blouse and black skirt, with black tights and shoes. However, her makeup was what you would call a Gothic look, terrifying with black lipstick, thick black eyeliner, huge artificial eyelashes flapping away, hair dyed jet black and put up with spider clips to match the scary look. We all stared in amazement at this apparition. Out of her hearing, someone joked that she was dressed for a funeral. She never smiled and walked around serving portions of food like a zombie.

The conversation began. Glaswegians are great storytellers and good listeners, never interrupting a long story. After it's told, they then add their own experiences on the subject. A lady began to talk about an area she stayed in as a child, called "The Haugh," situated around the docks on the River Clyde where ships docked from all over the world, a hive of activity. Mrs. Robertson's house was just up the road from there. The lady spoke of how tripe was sold door-to-door in years gone by, a man carrying a tin bath (the sort people washed in) before the advent of enamel baths or bathrooms. The tin bath was filled with tripe, sold in thin or thick slices, cheap enough to make a meal for a family with potatoes and onions. It was highly nutritious. The door-to-door salesmen were everywhere, some selling cleaning products, dusters, clothing, vacuum cleaners, and more. A lot of the men that sold around the doors were from India, Pakistan, the Caribbean, and other foreign countries. They provided a good service and made a good profit on the goods they sold. Glaswegians were generous when they had money to spend. My own grandmother was a great fan of tripe, but when I discovered it was from the lining of a sheep's stomach, I turned my nose up at the delicacy.

Everyone at the funeral table laughed heartily at the great tripe story, and it didn't turn us off our steak pies, served with seriousness by the Gothic waitress. I think the fact she was so serious made us laugh even more, maybe trying to cheer her up, but she kept her same look of sorrow.

The conversation then turned to the "rag and bone man," a man with a horse and cart loaded with clothes from all over the area. The horse always wore blinkers and was given a bag of oats to munch on, probably to stop him from annoying the umpteen kids that ran up to the cart with their old clothes, to swap them for a balloon or small toy, a treasure to kids who had nothing in the world to enjoy playing with

The man would blow a trumpet to announce his arrival. The excitement would be electric at the thought of a balloon or toy. The old man could tell who the poorer kids were and would still give them something even though they had no clothes to add to his cart. This was a great thrill in the 1950s when at the time I had only one jumper, the one on my back. The only snag about the rag man was that some kids were so excited to get something from him that one boy handed over his dad's Sunday best suit. Some were so desperate they could be seen taking off their socks, even in winter. We all had our own rag and bone story at the table. I wished I had taped the fun stories from all the great tales. The atmosphere at the table was so happy, with loud laughter. Nobody would have known we were at a funeral.

Another lady told a story of when she was a child, around five or six years old. When out playing with her pals, she saw three very drunk men walking down the street, all three with soft hats and coats on. The man in the center looked more drunk than the other two on either side of him. When she looked again, she realized that the center man was a side of beef (the huge carcasses that hung in butcher's shops at the time). It was the fact they all had the hats and coats on that was confusing to her. Obviously, it was two thieves stealing from a butcher's shop.

This story caused such a laugh among us all. The Gothic waitress appeared again with dessert.

Then George told the story of how he helped his friend Alex, whose parents owned a hotel on Argyll Street. He was asked to help out one night when they were short-staffed. George put on a waiter's white coat to serve guests at the hotel. The kind of people that stayed in hotels in those days had plenty of money and were mainly upper-class. Anyway, George went up to serve a couple of toffs at a table. He held a platter full of steak and gravy. As he lifted a spoonful of the food, a large chunk of steak landed in his white starched pocket. The coat was no longer white but had a dark brown gravy stain dripping down the area, causing shock to the two guests.

His next disaster was when opening a bottle of red wine with a corkscrew. The cork popped off and jumped into the wine glass of the guest. With aplomb, George stuck his finger into the glass and retrieved the unruly cork, then went ahead and poured the wine. Alex had seen George fish the cork from the glass with his finger. Talk about hygiene.

Again, the Gothic waitress appeared as we all enjoyed the tale of Faulty Towers in Glasgow. We nicknamed her Miss Lurch, as in "The Addams Family," a program on TV at that time.

Dessert was served as we all sat pretending to have straight, serious faces, just like the waitress. Someone said, as she walked out of hearing, "Does she have a pulse?" Another burst of laughter filled the table.

Then we got back to funeral talk. A guy had been at a funeral in Glasgow, and the service was in full flow, women grieving, men trying not to. The next thing, a mobile phone started to ring quite loudly. Everyone looked at the person next to them and realized the ringing sound was emanating from the coffin. Some wag said, "Did anyone say hello?" Serious stuff.

Partick sounded much rougher than Ibrox, where I was brought up. There was a man called "Shifty Young" who thought of a clever way to make some money. He tied a kid to a pole in the street and asked the parents for ransom.

George stayed in a posh close; it had an inside toilet, and they only had mice. Other closes had rats, he said seriously, telling this story.

Mrs. Robertson, his dear wee mum, worked in a sweet shop. Her husband had died, and she had to make ends meet. She had a box to stand on, as she was of small stature. One day, while standing on her box with a tray of sweets for all the kids who came into the shop that day, she fell on the floor. 1p caramels, jelly babies, sour plums, and other tasty stuff spread all over the floor. The kids were in heaven, grabbing them to eat before she chased them out of the shop.

Then came school talk. Some school in Partick had an English teacher who was an alcoholic. The kids had to go to the local pub between periods to drag him back to class for lessons.

My favorite story was about the "buffet." This was a new idea in the 1960s. Folk in Glasgow would try to copy the Southerners and serve small pieces of food on plates for guests to help themselves, or even posher, a grapefruit, not an orange, apple

CHAPTER 17

Garden

I had a long, hard, and heavy pregnancy. I had to leave work at only six months pregnant. I became huge in size and found any movement so painful; it was not like either of my previous pregnancies. I was older, my muscles were weaker, and I felt like I was carrying six bricks inside me. I had to be induced as I was overdue.

Eventually, after much pushing and shoving, out popped a little girl. I called her Heather-Iona. Andrew wanted her named Iona; I wanted Heather, so we decided on a hyphen to please us both. She was a big girl and screamed her head off for an hour after birth. I think the midwife had been a horse doctor in her previous job; she was as rough as they come, stitching me up with no lignocaine. I don't think she enjoyed her work, but thankfully, I recovered well.

The boys were off to America on Saturday to see their dad, so I thought it would be nice if they had a day with their new sister. I was home by Friday. Heather lay on the bed in my room, and her brothers came through to see her for the first time. It was thundering and lightning outside, and the new baby screamed her head off. Both boys just laughed at the scene, and Stuart christened her "Damian," like the horror film.

Heather is now 31 years old and anything but a Damian. She looks after Andrew and me, making sure we are well and helping with chores in the house. She is my angel from heaven, my right-hand girl. Although she has medical problems, she copes very well with them and carries on no matter what. Like us all, she has her bad points, but always asks for forgiveness when she gets annoyed. This I admire in her, as not many people today can say sorry; it's a word they find hard to use.

I have completed my story, not for fame, fortune, or self-satisfaction, nor to bring anyone down or cause hurt. More so, for all those out there in the world going through a breakup, marriage, or split from a partner. Remember, life is just a theater to teach our soul something. The real you is far more powerful than you would ever believe. You will get over a breakup. Like a death, it takes time, but always keep yourself strong and adjust to change in your life. The future is what you have manifested, so you can be happy again.

Scott married Jackie from Banff, a super lady. I am blessed with great daughter-in-laws. They have two lovely girls, Aurelia and Orlah, treasures from heaven. I see them every week, which is great in my old age. They so lift our spirits with laughter and joy.

Mrs. Millar died in Erskine Care Home. I did visit her and wished I had been in touch more. She had diabetes and a leg amputation. I was sad to hear of her death, but it felt like a blessing for her with no more pain. She was a truly lovely lady.

I never returned to nursing. I worked for a care company in Stonehaven Crossroads and also helped with Meals on Wheels. Eventually, I ended up working as a waitress in Dobbies Garden Centre Aberdeen. I loved my job but left in my 60s due to thyroid trouble. I still meet up with my Dobbies colleagues every month for a chat and lunch.

Today, I paint portraits and landscapes in oils, read lots of books about people's lives, and have an allotment where Andrew grows vegetables, and I grow flowers for bees and butterflies. I love my garden. I am interested in people who have had near-death experiences, how they have died and come back to tell what they experienced. At the moment, I'm reading Raymond Moody's book on life after life. I like to think that all my lovely patients that passed away are there in that heavenly place with their loved ones. I will always remember them all.

I hope my little book helps those going through a divorce or breakup with a partner, that they will be happy again. Life is just an experience, as I said earlier. It's important for yourself and your family to forgive and move on.

Alex and Mary married; Alex has three children, all of whom I look on as my dear grandchildren.

Eleven years ago, Stuart married a beautiful American lady, Nicole. Today, they have two children, Piper, 9, and Ewan, 2. They live in Chicago. I attended their wedding, as did Jim, his dad, my ex. When I arrived at the church, I sat at the entrance. Jim appeared and said there was a problem: "Who would walk down the aisle with him, as it was usually the parents of the groom?" I told him that was not a problem. I had arranged for an usher to walk with me, but here's a better idea: I would walk on one side of the usher, his new wife, Jeany, on the other, and he could walk behind. So, that's how we did it. Everyone had a puzzled look in the church as we walked down to the front, but my family had a giggle as they knew the story. "Love one another," as Jesus said.

THE END.

Printed in Great Britain
by Amazon

44474795R00076